Science and the Greys

L. Mason Jones served a number of years in the military, and travelling on a so-called 'government service' passport, found himself in such places as south Yemen, Bahrain, the Gulf of Oman, Cyprus and Germany. After leaving the service, he became part of the team producing the highly successful business jet, The Hawker 125. He functioned as a quality-engineering inspector with, initially, British Aerospace, then Corporate Jets Inc, and finally Raytheon USA. The latter purchased the thriving business and moved production to the USA. Mr Jones then left the business to concentrate on writing projects. He has three adult offspring and resides in Chester.

Works by the same author:

Modern Ancients, 2023

Strange Realities, 2021

The Human Enigma, 2021

Cultural Shock, 2020

When the Moon Came, 2020

Pillars of Fire, 2019

Monkey Trial, 2019

SCIENCE AND THE GREYS

L. MASON JONES

Arena Books

Copyright © L. Mason Jones 2024

The right of L. Mason Jones to be identified as the author of this work has been asserted in accordance with the Copyright, Design and Patents Act 1988.

First published by Arena Books in 2024

www.arenabooks.co.uk

All rights reserved. Except for the quotation of short passages for the purposes of criticism and review, no part of this publication may be reproduced, stored in a retrieval system, or transmitted, in any form or by any means, electronic, mechanical, photocopying, or recording or otherwise, without prior permission of the publisher.

L. Mason Jones
Science and the Greys

British Library cataloguing in Publication Data. A Catalogue record for this book is available from the British Library.

ISBN: 978-1-914390-27-2 Paperback
ISBN: 978-1-914390-28-9 Ebook

Thema: JBG; VXQB

Cover design by Arena Books

Contents

CHAPTER I: SCIENCE AND THE GREYS   1

CHAPTER II: THE CHURCH AND THE GREYS   97

CHAPTER III: ABDUCTIONS AND THE GREYS   135

BIBLIOGRAPHY   173

CHAPTER I

SCIENCE AND THE GREYS

It is fairly certain that all members of the sciences are well aware of what the term 'the Greys' means and its implications for humanity. This is simply because various members of their group have dealt with, and have come into close contact with, the very people who gave this name to the creatures who now bear this title.

The various branches of science who have been involved with the phenomenon of human abductions by unearthly beings include the medical sciences, psychiatrists, hypnotherapists, astronomers, surgeons, cosmologists and astro-biologists. But it is clear that we not only need to research the 'abductors' themselves, but also their methods of travelling about our globe. So the study of their craft (that have commonly been called 'UFOs') must also be included in any meaningful study of the entire phenomenon.

Just to imagine that humanoid living entities have traversed the gulf of space, found our world, and are currently studying all the flora and fauna of our planet including humans in some kind of operating theatre within their craft, is an utterly fantastic conception. However, it does not stop there. Many people actually believe that these beings and their predecessors actually discovered our world during our distant past, and may actually have been responsible for the higher qualities of creativity and intelligence that human beings possess. This theory puts forward the idea that it is these extra-terrestrials who set us on the road to becoming 'creators' and who may actually enable us to become interstellar travellers ourselves in the future.

As fantastic as it may sound, there is nothing in this seemingly science-fiction-like theory that could make it impossible to accept. Our geneticists and astro-biologists may well agree on this point. As may some of our paleoanthropologists, who may accept that it goes some way to explaining the many gaps in the natural selection process of the human from a primate creature. Nevertheless, for all that, there are many members of the sciences who totally reject the whole idea of such a concept. But the idea cannot simply be disregarded, they must offer sound reasons for rejecting the possibility. The United States is a big country, so it should not be surprising that such a huge number of people claim that they have been involved with this phenomenon. But we must also remember that claims of alien abductions and/or close encounters with objects that could hardly be terrestrial in their amazing aerodynamic displays, exist all over the world. So how does this phenomenon, in particular the so called Greys, sit with science? Why the description 'grey' in the first place? The answer to the first question is that science has many alternative explanations that allows it to reject it, or dismiss it as the 'Spielberg effect.' And conversely, the vast majority of the general public have allowed themselves to discount the idea that other explanations are possible, such as optical illusions, meteors, satellites, and so forth. Aided and abetted by frightening films of an alien takeover, people formulate the concept that extra-terrestrials are about to conquer the Earth and take it for themselves. Thereby, a form of mass hysteria among the population is created and everyone accepts the idea of ETs as dangerous. It has to be said that this is a very important point when considering this phenomenon. Humans can very quickly be sent out of control by fear; this was demonstrated when the dramatic version of H G Wells' *War of the Worlds* was broadcast on the radio in 1938. Many people who had not heard the programme from the beginning believed that Martians had arrived to conquer the world. As for the second question regarding the description of these alleged entities as 'grey', this is due to the fact that all the descriptions given by the alleged victims of the abductions have described their skin as resembling this particular hue.

One important reason that science cannot simply disregard the possibility that these beings exist, is because the early members of their profession are responsible for the belief in the first place. Ever since the learned Greeks, and down through the centuries of scientific thought, scientists have pondered the question of other living planets and the other living creatures that may populate them. Some of these scientists and thinkers paid with their lives for such pronouncements.

With regard to the aforementioned director Stephen Spielberg, he was very good at his job at producing good films dealing with extra-terrestrials. And in actual fact, not all of his films on the topic were negative depictions. He actually also introduced a different concept with regard to their main intentions, which was one of a more friendly nature. By contrast, most films before this, guided by our own human nature of war, aggression and conquering other nations, were all about how extra-terrestrials were out to conquer and destroy us.

Unfortunately, this attitude, which is quite worrisome, still seems to exist in the minds of those scientists and technicians who are developing methods and ways of sending "ET back to where he came from." Such statements clearly indicate that we have, over the centuries, learned nothing, but still retain the concept that any creatures 'not of this Earth' would wish only to conquer the world.

It would seem that visiting ETs would have been more welcome in the days of Newton and his type, as opposed to the scientists who now work behind the scenes with the group who hold back all the classified information from the rest of us. The possibility that we are not alone in the universe is a subject that mankind has pondered for centuries. A good proportion of the blame for the idea that other world beings would want to conquer us must be laid at the door of H G Wells and other film writers of his type. However, it did not seem that the ancient philosophers who pondered the subject deeply, thought in those terms. In the days of the great thinkers, mathematicians and geographers of ancient Greece, genius and high intelligence seems to have been present in a higher proportion of the population. And of course, we would have to say the same with regard to the ancient Egyptians who taught the Greeks so much.

These were the kinds of people that Isaac Newton referred to when he stated, "If I have seen further, it is because I have stood on the shoulders of giants." He would no doubt have included Johannes Kepler as one of these 'giants', because it was Kepler from whom Newton learned so much when he was formulating his theories of gravity and its relevance to the universe.

Of course, long before Newton's time, scientifically orientated people had to be very careful with their discoveries, and what their discoveries implied, and more importantly, who they related their discoveries to, for fear of persecution. When considering all these known factors, and our amazing scientific advancements of today, the fact that some scientists can disregard this rather profound phenomenon as being all down to human fallibility is quite surprising.

In the factual film, *Battle of the Bulge*, a middle ranking officer who had been a police inspector, tries to convince the top brass that the Germans were going to attack. But he is derided and told "All my officers think differently" and (in rather basic terms) is told, "When ten men tell you, you are drunk, then you had better lie down."

When tens of thousands of people tell science that they have experienced a phenomenon that could only be described as 'out of this world,' and many thousands more swear that they have been taken aboard an alien craft and poked about, then science ought not to lie down but 'listen up', and give more credence to a phenomenon that cries out for serious scientific study. It ought not to be derided or disregarded. Moreover, it would actually be a very worrying fact, and also worthy of study, if such a high portion of the population had simply imagined it all. After all, the explanations are rather strange; being rendered into a somnambulistic condition, then taken by small humanoid creatures into an alien craft, placed on an operating table, and being subjected to medical procedures. It is a rather profound occurrence for science to accept without question, but look into it they must.

If one thinks that this phenomenon is strange, then what about an alleged occurrence (that we will deal with later) in which a lady was floated out of her top storey window and beamed up by the Greys into a huge UFO? Yet, the phenomenon of unidentified flying objects is impossible for science to disregard when it involves people of very high standing such as priests, presidents and even a pope.

In any case, indisputably, extra-terrestrials in the form of humans have descended themselves onto another world. Our Moon is seen as being far too large, compared to the other satellites in the solar system, to be classified as a satellite. Instead, it is part of a double planetary system with the Earth. We humans have played the part of extra-terrestrial by landing upon it and if 'little grey men' occupy its interior, as has been suggested, then we as an advanced space travelling lifeform would ultimately have to confront and come to terms with these inhabitants or 'Selenites'. And so it must be for the visiting entities alleged to be present on our own world. However, scientific opinion varies greatly with the entire phenomenon and in particular with the alleged abductions. But they must recognise the fact that it is an issue that exists and they cannot avoid the fact that it has been with us for some time and must ultimately be resolved or at least faced up to. When we mentioned Isaac Newton and his declaration of having 'stood on the shoulders of giants,' so indeed did the ancient Greeks with regard to the archaic Egyptians and their amazing achievements and technological knowledge.

For quite some time, links of a cosmic, celestial and often extra-terrestrial nature have been made with regard to ancient Egyptian culture. This would naturally occur, if the rather profound theory that the predecessors of the creatures we know as the Greys were actively involved in the genetic procedures to make modern humans. As this amazing proposition would mean that thousands of years (of our time) would have passed since the so-called 'cultural evolution' of the human entity. This would, of course, mean that the greys, if they exist in our earth space, would be responsible for all the references to 'gods', angels and any mysterious individuals with special powers.

The pinnacle of Egyptian achievement are the mysterious and enigmatic pyramids, and although we are learning so much about them, they still retain many of their mysteries. When scientists reflect on their own achievements, they must surely realise, particularly with regard to their vast cosmic knowledge and advancements in space activity, that they are rushing headlong into the situation where humans themselves will become the ET visitors to other worlds. In this scenario, in the far distant future, if we encounter sentient beings with limited intelligence, then perhaps they will deride each other and dismiss those who encounter us as cranks or 'a bit odd.'

If we discovered other worlds, would we then, in our turn, consider using our advanced knowledge to enhance biological life forms, genetics, and all the medical expertise to help them to advance? Most certainly! We would initially be very careful about being easily seen in their skies, but this could not be completely avoided. We think we can be sure that a mission of furtive abductions of their body forms would begin, and the process would almost certainly follow that which we believe could be happening on our own planet today.

We must also consider that future human astronauts would, once this process had begun, bear a great burden of responsibility toward the beings we may discover. And no matter how long the process continued, there would be a conclusion, a final plan, and revelations once we were sure that they could accept the knowledge that we could impart.

This could quite easily reflect on what we, as humans, now face on Earth. If it comes to pass that we discover that we were, in the long distant past, genetically 'modified', then these factors would eventually be revealed to us, and we, in turn, would pick up the baton. After all, there must be a more profound reason for this great gift of intelligence than travelling off into the cosmos just out of curiosity; we would have a duty to 'bear the burden of creation' and to enhance intelligence in living creatures elsewhere in space.

We have said in another work, if ET is coursing through our skies and astounding the witnesses with their manoeuvres and what they are capable of, this need not generate fear, especially if we simply postulate on what we have said, with what we ourselves may eventually be capable of. They cannot hide their technology and capabilities and neither would we be able to.

We would have to be very careful how we went about our operations and ensure that we did not alarm the occupants of the discovered world. This reaction may not necessarily be automatic. After all, in pre-Columban times, when the north and south Americans met the pale-faced ones, they did not fear their obvious technology and run from it. On the contrary, they brought gifts and welcomed the strange visitors. This was more noticeable among the South Americans as the coming of the white men coincided with a prediction of a certain individual who was accepted as a 'god', simply returning with a host of others, as he had promised.

Is this not akin to the promised Christian 'second coming' also involving beings accepted as gods (or angels)? The resentment among the north and south American Indians only came later when they realised the true intentions of the 'visitors'. In our case however, since we had already possessed these characteristics, people such as the aforementioned H G Wells and other writers assumed that this is how strange beings coming to our world would behave. And who could blame him? After all, he lived in an era of Victorian grandeur and expansion, and during a time when the domineering of other races occurred through colonial expansion and the coveting of the resources of subdued lands.

However, we could add that as far as the people of these lands were concerned, much was given along with what was taken; political organisations, democracy in place of tribalism, improved roads, education, railways, and so forth. And so, it was not all bad news for the occupants of the subdued people and their lands. In a sense, this may also come about if we made the right decision, with regard to our (obviously advanced) hypothetical 'grey visitors'. Clearly, as we have said, the strongest factor in regard to this non-belligerence is that if they only had subjugation and the conquering of the Earth in mind, then they would have done this long ago. Furthermore, in pursuance of this theory, why would they wait for so many centuries (assuming the Biblical events were the original Greys) until we had developed our defence weapons from spears to missiles? If people were subjected to these kinds of thoughts and ideas, then surely a gradual realisation that having a great fear of such creatures would be totally unnecessary. What we need is a prolonged (sermon if you like) of instilling these thoughts into the minds of the people and science should certainly encourage the idea of this process. This obviously highlights the hiding of such information, which we assume is to do with our 'grey visitors' as being totally unnecessary, but we would encourage the idea that the programme should include the heads of the Church and involve all the various faiths and we will pursue this suggestion in the chapter dealing with 'The Church and the Greys'.

If the security group, who only release the information that they decide we can be made aware of and nobody else, they would obviously have a certain group of chosen scientists working with them, some of whom would have highly tuned telepathic receiving capabilities which many of us have but are not fully aware of it.

This would afford full dialogue in order to be able to work with them, such as the individual who made the statement "We will soon have the capability to send ET back where he came from" and possibly many others who make these so outdated and belligerent remarks. These would be quite an embarrassment to those in this secretive group who are liaising with the Greys. The latter might be concerned about such language, and one could imagine the possible reply from the humans in the secretive group. Perhaps they would reassure the Greys by saying, "Don't worry, we will take care of them later." This may go a little further than simply sending the 'men in black' to make veiled threats to them.

Even many scientists who were involved with our 'embryo' space programme since the fifties, could not seem to grasp the idea that other intelligences may have surpassed us in our space-travelling efforts – perhaps centuries, or even thousands of years, before we even began. One such member was Edward Condon, who in his report, considered the entire UFO phenomena and the possible occupants of such craft as "Not worth investigating." He did not see it as having any bearing on the advancement of science.

This is quite astounding on reflection, as it clearly suggests that although he was aware of what humans could achieve, nobody else other than 'earthlings' could do so. It seems Dr Condon was not open to 'conversion.' But another scientist who initially took the same view as Doctor Condon was thoroughly converted simply because, rather than just evaluating written data on the phenomenon, he witnessed the 'sharp end', so to speak; he became overwhelmed by the mass of very convincing data and verbally transmitted accounts from visibly shocked and traumatised witnesses. He could not help but formulate the opinion that the phenomenon was a real issue to be scientifically dealt with. This gentleman made it his mission profile to convince mainstream science that we have a highly important issue to deal with and that the sooner we get to grips with it, the better. We refer, of course, to the late Dr J. Allen Hynek. He addressed a scientific group with this objective in mind.

It may seem strange to some other members of science who are sympathetic to the ET hypothesis and the UFO phenomena that with such an overwhelming and quite massive amount of data and very reliable witness reports, there are still many scientists who oppose the reality of the issue. Of course, they are entitled to their opinion. After all, it is quite a fantastic concept to grasp. Nevertheless, humanity has long been exposed to the possibility through the media, films, books and news reports, not only in modern times but through philosophic pronouncements, made over the decades (if not generations) that humans cannot possibly be the pinnacle of creation and the only intelligent beings with space travelling ambitions in the vast wondrous universe. This would simply defy all logic.

With regard to the long-established viewpoint on celestial matters, we find it quite incredible to imagine how such archaic people as the Ancient Egyptians could possibly be aware of the environment of outer space. A good example of this is a certain ancient Egyptian papyrus that we referred to in my book *Strange Realities*. This refers to an extract from the Egyptian *Book of the Dead* which reads, "This place has no air, its depth is unfathomable, and it is as black as the blackest of nights." How could the writer possibly have known this? It is clearly describing the depths of space. This profound information could only have been taught (or possibly experienced) by the writer, who clearly recorded it as established facts and not in terms of a theory or a supposition. But we have to wonder who was the tutor? Space scientists should be quite astounded by such statements as these from antiquity, as the people of those times should only have been aware of the earthly environment. In fact, people and the primitive science of many centuries later envisaged 'air' as reaching all the way to the Moon. They even reflected on undertaking balloon trips there and possibly even tried it. If nothing else, such undertakings must have contributed inadvertently to our early knowledge of space medicine, and to the thinning of the air with altitude, loss of air pressure, and so-forth.

Although the Romans were known predominately as ruthless conquerors, they did bring very advanced engineering methods and technology to other lands, just as (as we have mentioned) the British did in their empirical expansion. They also, like the Greeks before them, produced their fair share of great minds, philosophers, poets and historians and avidly contributed to our knowledge of them today.

We have said, for all that, regarding the ancient British peoples, we had our fair share of such enlightened minds, but they remained very much in the shade in comparison to our occupiers. However, all of this changed, of course, when the Romans finally left Britain and a renaissance of our own enlightened ones began to take effect and they began to re-establish themselves. But the vacuum was also filled by the noticeable flowering of Christianity, which had always been present, but in a more subdued fashion. When the Romans themselves began to embrace Christianity, and even produce an Emperor who converted to the faith, the Church's power knew no bounds and it is for certain that if any of its subjects made any references to outer space in the form of which we quoted from the Egyptian *Book of the Dead*, the consequences for them could have been dire. And so, when the great pagan nation of Rome weakened its grip, an even stronger grip was applied to the threats of anyone who exercised their right to what we would call today 'free speech.' And so, the Church used an abused its power almost as severely as the Romans did to anyone who broke Caesar's Law.

Now it was the turn of the Abbeys and monasteries and the learned and educated monks, who became great historians of the land, but even they were not immune from the wrath of the Church if they did not guard their tongue; we have mentioned what happened to Giordano Bruno, who envisaged outer space, and other worlds with people on them, much like ourselves. In our minds, we have come to imagine monks as moving slowly along in a line, chanting or voicing prayers, hands clasped, head bowed, or kneeling and praying before the altar. They did these things for sure, but they were proficient gardeners, builders, were highly intelligent. Unlike others in the population, they could write and used this skill in recording all they knew for posterity. They filled many gaps with regard to our knowledge of post Roman Britain.

There is a strange paradox here when we consider that they spent much, if not all of their lives, being incarcerated within their cloistered environments and yet they attained and wrote of all this knowledge. One would have thought that with all these restrictions on them, that they would be ill-informed of such knowledge of what was going in the wider world. But their writings were beautifully artistic, beginning with a large multicoloured capitol letter followed by enlightened prose in leather-bound volumes that lasted all down through the ages. As well as religious works and historical data, they sometimes speculated on things that were outside of their remit and such writings must have been known by science and raised a few eyebrows. They spoke of celestial and cosmic subjects known only fairly recently, gained by our own scientific cosmic knowledge. Of course, such speculative writings (such as the aforementioned Giordano Bruno) would have been heavily dampened down due to the fear of the ecclesiastic hierarchy who would soon descend upon those who wrote of things that would only be seen as 'machinations of the devil.' Burning a person alive must have been the most horrific thing a human can do to another (with the possible flaying of the skin, which was also done), yet the supposedly pious overseers coolly ignored the commandment 'thou shalt not kill' and watched one of their own suffer this terrible fate.

Yet, even before Bruno, the ancient Greeks were considering such things as other worlds, and intelligences in existence far from our own world. Certainly, these were the kinds of people that Newton referred to and on whose shoulders he stood in order to see further. Bruno was given the chance to recant, but because of his strength of character, he refused and was 'murdered' (there is no other word for it) by the Elders. They could just as easily have imprisoned him, but they chose to sit in Holy Robes and watch him die a horrific death. How things have changed. The Vatican now has its own observatory and certainly now agrees with Bruno's proclamation, "There are an infinite number of suns in the universe with planets that revolve around them and that some of these worlds might be populated." Science has had many centuries in which to contemplate the possible existence of other intelligent life in space, which of course is proven by our own existence here on Earth and we are all well aware of the intensive efforts being made by the S.E.T.I programme to find them. After all this, it is quite disconcerting to find that some members of science reject the idea of other life existing off Earth, and any possibility of anyone else having discovered our planet, when such a countless abundance of signs have been given to us short of their actual appearance.

Yet, there is this dark curtain of secrecy that has descended and separated not only the public, but science itself, into two factions – those who know, and those who merely surmise. And those who know make a determined effort to prevent those who surmise from thinking otherwise. And so, in spite of all the proclamations and prophesies and enlightening data in the past and the obvious conclusions as to where it will end with regard to our own space ambitions, there still exists this hard group of scientists who will totally refute the idea. The former sceptic, Dr J Allen Hynek, made it his mission to convince the sceptics among the scientific fraternity, and became known as the 'guru' of all things celestial. He tried to encourage other sceptics to face up to the reality regarding the subject.

Another guru of all things cosmic was Isaac Newton who brought law

SCIENCE AND THE GREYS

and order to the universe with his proclamations on gravity – that great universal force that controls everything that moves in the cosmos. The great physicists, with their intense studies of matter and its atomic structure, were all quite aware of this force that controls all the atomic particles rushing around in circles within a pinhead as well as a planet. As are their descendants who have taken the great discoveries so much further and who now delve into the mysteries of quantum physics which can make one's head reel and bring us ever closer together with their partners at C.E.R.N to the secrets of life itself and trying to touch the face of God.

And so, people like Dr Hynek and others like him such as the more recent Dr Greer, attempt to lift the dark blanket of disbelief from the heads of those existing among the science fraternity. They attempt to enlighten who despite freely admitting that one day ETs in the form of humans will move around the atmosphere of another earth-like world being careful not to alarm the occupants too dramatically, still refute all possibility of such a thing happening on our own planet.

The title of one of my books, *High Strangeness*, was a phrase used by the aforementioned Dr Hynek with regard to some of the cases he dealt with. Dr Hynek had experienced the traumatic effects on people of all positions, and all walks of life, who had been deeply affected by their experiences with this phenomenon – in particular the alleged human abductions. In his day, he was possibly the most important scientist who took the matter seriously. But there were also other scientists who quietly accepted the reality of these phenomena but were not prepared, for their own reasons, to raise their profile and 'come in from the cold.'

The once widely used term 'little green men' was often accompanied by a snigger or two. Of course, today there are no reports of little green men being seen (if there ever were), but there are plenty of reports regarding 'little grey men.' This is not a colour fashion trend but due to the immense amount of worldwide abduction claims. Yet it still involves a certain amount of sceptical amusement. The strange paradox exists within science that although some will laugh at the possible existence of these creatures, there are other members of their profession who state that long into the future, humans may well resemble this body form themselves. Dr Hynek was more than qualified to deeply involve himself, with a few others, into this important issue of the UFO phenomenon – and especially with the living entities associated with it who we refer to as the Greys. He was a former chairman of The Department of Astronomy at North Western University in the US. His deep analysis of the issue caused him to conclude that we had a very real phenomenon to deal with and that we had to approach it and come to terms with it in a serious manner.

This would need the involvement not only of scientists in the USA, but all around the world – since cases existed and had been investigated around the world. The problem, however, was that when it was attempted, it was almost always carried out by self-funded volunteer groups rather than by scientists who largely tended to distance themselves from the issue. Dr Hynek could not stress enough the fact that these phenomena demanded serious scientific attention. In particular, as the cases of close encounters with alleged UFO and also claims of ET abductions seemed to be increasing rather than diminishing.

However, for all that, rather lame and dismissive reasons were continually trotted out by science in order to escape the need for profound examination of each individual case. Dr Hynek was in a position to understand this attitude, as he himself had been commissioned by the US Air Force to do just that. There was a pretence of involving science into the investigations to give it an air of attention. As time went on, Dr Hynek felt more and more like a fraud as he knew the seriousness of the subject and could no longer trot out the usual explanations despite the Air Force expecting that of him.

Dr Hynek had got a little tired of the usual explanations of nocturnal lights, ball lightning, satellites, meteors and swamp gas, but it was he himself who mentioned this latter possibility in one case. And so 'swamp gas' became a godsend to the debunkers who seized upon it, along with the weather balloons theory, to explain every case. The public by and large saw through this subterfuge and became somewhat irritated by it and this do doubt gave rise to the many private organisations that began to emerge in order to get to grips with the issues. But their means were limited and substantial funds had to be found in order to cover travel costs, hotels, and so-forth. Dr Hynek admitted that the people he initially worked for did everything they could to downgrade the importance of all the cases in which they could get away with it.

Dr Hynek felt that his reputation had been somewhat diminished as so many people associated with him with the 'swamp case' explanation. The result of all this was that Hynek was armed with an abundance of case files, many of which he had personally investigated and published in various books and magazines. He supported the view that "This whole U.F.O business takes us to the edge of reality in that it represents an unknown, but real, phenomenon that demands the most serious scientific attention that is currently not taking place." This was the scientific turning point for Hynek. He would no longer be the scientific debunker for the Air Force.

However, one cannot help but sympathise with the Air Force as they could not allow the public to assume that they could no longer protect them from an unknown technology in the skies (which, in fact, they could not). One has to know an alleged enemy in order to formulate a defence plan and they simply did not know. They didn't even know if the phenomenon was an enemy, let alone on how to deal with it.

They could not portray a situation where they appeared helpless in the face of the 'threat' (which many people thought that it was) due entirely to a barrage of science-fiction films such as *Earth Versus the Flying Saucers*, *War of the Worlds* and so forth. Therefore, the only option open to the Air Force was to dismiss the phenomena and make the population assume that it was all their own fault through overly vivid imaginations. This had the opposite effect to what was intended. Many of those (and there were many) who had experienced the unexplainable felt quite insulted by this 'slur' on their integrity and demanded a more serious study of the problem. Of course, behind the scenes, a frantic series of meetings was taking place by the Defence Department. One of the more serious suggestions was made after a large group of UFOs flew over Washington, the Whitehouse, and other no-fly areas with impunity. The suggestion was made that the Soviets could mount a sneak attack and prevent retaliation if they used the UFO phenomena to annihilate all the major cities in the US together with the missile silos. Many and varied possible situations were formulated that made the Secret Service and the Military form an elite group who were no doubt the forerunners of the so-called 'faceless ones' we are aware of today – those who are impervious to any Freedom of Information Laws.

However, rather than behind the scenes, people such as Dr Hynek were quite out in the open with regard to their objective, which, as said, was to encourage a serious investigation of this phenomenon. As well as being a professional astronomer, he was also the chairman and director of the McMillin Observatory of Ohio State University. During his chairmanship here, he addressed a meeting with the Optical Society of America and quickly came to the point with his audience. He soon made it clear that it was no longer fashionable to be sceptical with regard to the phenomena we have been discussing. He pointed out that those scientists who had suggested that the entire phenomenon was simply a psychological issue brought on by films, books, and hysteria, were condemning a huge portion of the US population as being of unsound mind.

He made the point that the phenomenon was too vast to be simply written off as being the result of people's overactive imaginations. However, he also made it clear that there were indeed some people who he referred to as 'kooks and nuts.' After making it clear that unidentified flying objects, even their alleged small grey occupants, demands serious investigation, he added, "I say this from the start, so that you are not misled by the kooks, the nuts and the gullible, who have made this subject so difficult to explore rationally. UFOs are a real puzzle. The idea of a myth is long put to rest and the scientific community must now take much more cognisance of them." Since all of this took place decades ago, it shows just how long science has been encouraged and under pressure to take the subject seriously. Yet still today, those that do appear outspoken on the possible reality of the phenomenon are side-lined as mavericks or looked on as fans of the paranormal. Nevertheless, there are many PhDs and professors among their ranks. During his strenuous efforts to make the science fraternity sit up and pay attention, Dr Hynek held other important posts to do with space operations and things of a cosmic nature.

For example, he was in charge of the optical satellite tracking programme of the Smithsonian Astrophysical Observatory in Cambridge, Massachusetts and certainly knew his satellites from UFOs, which are continually offered as explanations for many of the sightings.

The renaissance of the 'ancient astronaut' topic and various contributory TV programmes dealing with it have brought to light the significance of certain areas and bases in the US that are continually linked with the subject. These include the Lockheed Martin Skunk works, Area 51, Wright Pattison Air Force Base, and so forth. The latter is involved in foreign technology and an established department there is said to house parts of UFOs as well as bodies of the alleged 'grey entities' that originated from the well- known 1947 Roswell incident where such bodies were said to have been recovered.

Although at one point Dr Hynek held a post there, he never mentioned in what capacity he functioned in. He naturally had a very high security classification, but would have been sworn to secrecy. He spent some eighteen years of his life as scientific consultant to the Air Force and in that regard he must have encountered some very highly classified evidence and data. Nevertheless, although he did not agree with the Air Force's policy of pretence and keeping the public in the dark, he was a loyal US citizen and not a 'whistle blower' to use modern parlance. He would have known that secrecy was not only all about UFOs and 'little grey men', but was also about keeping ahead with regard to defence equipment – and staying ahead of any prospective foe. After all, in spite of our claims of being a highly advanced civilisation, our behaviour with regard to defence, attack, and warfare has not changed in any real way since the days of Alexander the Great or the Roman Legions.

During his time with the US Air Force as their scientific spokesman, he is said to have studied over ten thousand case files, many of which he had personally investigated himself. He felt that it was his duty to urge science to take it seriously, probably so that they would assist in preparing the people to face up to the possible reality of the phenomena rather than just putting his own head on the block, so to speak. So, if he succeeded in this objective, he would be in a 'safety in numbers situation', as he was well aware of all the claims of alleged assassinations of anyone inside the loop who stepped outside of it. And the ufologists are well aware of this and claim in a 'conspiracy programme,' that the late Defence Secretary of the US, James Forrestal, was one such victim. When Dr Hynek spoke to the aforementioned group of scientists, engineers and technicians of the Optical Society, he admitted that he was originally a sceptic himself and that he originally thought that the whole subject would simply 'go up in smoke.' But the phenomena has not gone away, in fact is had intensified. Hynek made it clear to them, "There are many persons of high status and with impressive qualifications who are preparing all aspects of this phenomena in quite an articulate manner and deserve to be listened to."

We have mentioned in another work that Dr Hynek was berated by a leading scientist of a top-ranking university for not 'coming out,' before this and clearly stating that, "These so-called UFOs had to be extra-terrestrial." And he was asked, "Can we not accept this as a fact today?" We do not know what Hynek's reply was, but we would suggest that it ought to have been, "Well why did you not come forward yourself and say so, if that is what you believed, instead of leaving me with the burden of applying the pressure to our own fellow members to face up to the issue. I would have been grateful for some support. Too many of our kind are thinking in the same way but not speaking out."

As Hynek continued his address to the Optical Society, he admitted that when shedding his scepticism, "I could do little else other than to bow down to the sheer volume of evidence provided by competent and highly qualified people across a broad band of occupations and positions, even the head of the Roman Catholic Church, Pope Pius XII was not exempt. He had a close encounter in the Vatican gardens in 1950. For all we know today, such an intensive scientific study may well have occurred in secret, but if so, our mainstream science is not aware of it. If, as we suspect, the faceless security operators are working with the Greys, then there would be no necessity for it.

However, we will proceed on the assumption that such an intensive study has not taken place and that many people would wish that it should and that it ought to include definite scientific study by university researchers. It should include computer analysis of any potential patterns that may emerge by evaluating all the available data up to the latest cases. The privately funded UFO groups have a mass of data in their case files that could be accessed by those who would take on the task, and something positive may well emerge from it all. Such a team would expect to be fully staffed, and, most importantly, government-funded in a properly set up research centre.

Scientists like Dr Hynek have made it clear that, "it is entirely possible that a scientific breakthrough could be achieved and that science would be neglecting its responsibility by not fulfilling such an operation. Every avenue must be explored," and that "ridicule is no longer acceptable, appropriate, or necessary." Most of the American public are aware, even though it took place decades ago, that a great chance was missed. Some researchers described it as little more than a sham. It was carried out in the guise of a serious study.

Dr Hynek was well aware of this, as he was part of it. It was, allegedly, the only 'serious' study that had taken place, although the UFO phenomena and speculation with regard to the Greys had been prevalent for some twenty years previously – ever since the dramatic days of 1947. Various projects took place, such as project 'Sign' and project 'Blue Book' and then the lengthy Condon Report. Dr Hynek had been involved in all of them. All these projects were somewhat flawed right from the start by being composed largely of sceptical individuals.

The unfortunate Hynek was, in a sense, 'used' to portray an air of scientifically serious analysis of the issue. Certain members of the teams set up to try to diminish the importance of the phenomenon. As such, many of those who reported strange encounters and experiences were subjected to ridicule. However, as it was pointed out by Dr Hynek and others, the investigating team brought a certain amount of ridicule on themselves by carrying out so many 'lukewarm' investigations.

Some examples of this were stating that the victim had simply observed the planet Venus, when at that time it was not observable in the night sky. Or, stating that they had simply seen a weather balloon when none had been launched, and so forth. They reinforced these rather weak explanations to formulate the conclusion that the subject was simply not worth pursuing and certainly not worth considering as any kind of threat to the defence of the country. The message was that people should stop worrying and relax, yet all the time behind the scenes, they knew that the issue was a serious matter.

However, as we have said, what else could they say? "Yes, we know that the phenomenon exists, but we don't know what to do about it"? Consider the chaos and riotous upheaval that would ensue. Nevertheless, the evidence is plain to see by the project director himself, which was a certain Robert J Low. This gentleman issued a memo (rather naively one might say) that he must have known would go on file, in which he said, "The 'trick' would be, I think, to describe the project so that, to the public, it would 'appear' to be a totally objective study but to science it would project the image of a group of 'non believers' trying their best to be objective."

To put this in a nutshell, one might describe it as 'let's pretend'. However, this trick was alleged to have cost the US taxpayer dearly. The figure was later estimated to be over half a million dollars, which of course would be substantially more in modern day costs, probably around four million dollars or more.

The whole principle behind the project was to dampen down public hysteria, but everyone knows how quickly public hysteria can flare up again. Modern day events have seen an abundance of human rioting and destructive behaviour over issues far less serious than the revelations of UFOs and humanoid beings, actually existing on Earth whose intentions may not be strictly honourable.

One cannot help being sympathetic to a degree for the authorities that are in a very difficult (one might almost say) no-win situation. However, whichever way we look at it, what must be, must be, There is no point in hiding the facts, as seems to be the case, surely the best way to proceed is just what we have suggested in the work, a slow process of revelations preferably handled by the Church.

One might suppose that it would be against the true beliefs of science to hide away facts rather than to face up to them, evaluate them and deal with them. Nevertheless, many scientists must be working with, and going along with all the subterfuge, secrecy and keeping those that they have decided to have no 'need to know' in the dark. For all that, the head of the aforesaid operation to ignore the facts and serious reports as mentioned above was a nuclear physicist, yet his primary role was to relieve the pressure on the US Air Force.

A nuclear physicist of an earlier age, that is, the New Zealander Ernest Rutherford, won the Nobel Prize for splitting the atom in 1931. All those wrapped up in the secrets of matter and the search for the secrets of life itself and great advances in the field of physics have been made since those times. it seems quite certain that the sciences of physics, genetics, biology and medical science would be delighted to study extra-terrestrial life forms (if allowed to). The cellular makeup, alien biology and distribution of the organs and methods of reproduction, the facts of their evolution and all the data regarding an 'other world' being. This could be achieved if science was at the forefront of encouraging, along with the Church, the futility, not to mention stupidity in adopting the ancient belligerence and fear of the unknown, by encouraging any military action against a lifeform simply by assuming that they would think like ourselves and are only out to conquer the Earth.

If the Greys are among us, their natural advanced intellect would make them realise that the human appears to be totally unable to handle any contact with their life forms at the present and for the Greys, that is their greatest dilemma. It could well be that they may decide simply to depart, to watch us from afar and delay the decision to make contact until we are about to travel outside our solar system. If, by that time, human behaviour patterns and the ingrained militaristic tendencies have not abated, then a major decision would have to be made with regard to the human species - who might be seen as the most dangerous species in the galaxy. Those who accept that humans now have the advanced capability (kindly provided by the predecessors of the Greys) to re-tune our brains' negative activities, would naturally expect us to exercise this ability and prepare us to be fit and ready to enter the cosmic brotherhood, but not declare war on it.

However, we have a long way to go before we reach that point, so the dilemma still exists and we can only guess at the possible outcome, but all of this does entail a lot of assumptions, so let us begin with the root cause of it, which is not conjecture but fact, and that is, vital and profound information is clearly being withheld from mainstream humanity. The reasons why, are debatable and some quite valid, but just to 'pretend' to inform us and by this method, by taking the trouble to produce a bulky book of hundreds of pages long, that is of very little value, is one way to do it. Another is to release hundreds of pages of worthless documents, since most of the text is ruled through, thereby pretending to release all the facts demanded by the Freedom of Information Laws does not add up to much by way of informing the public of a phenomenon that could be more profound and startling than any revelations so far pronounced.

The aforesaid book formerly known as the 'Condon Report', dwelt purposely on reports of alleged encounters with strange craft and the occupants that were obviously suspect and quite easily explained away and therefore held little interest to people making an effort to plough through it, but the overall impression was just as it was meant to be, that a major effort had been made with the involvement of science to study and analyse the issue that required to be dealt with.

The primary factor here is that the people that produce all this data, are addressing a nation where around ninety-four per cent of its members are aware of, read of, or even experienced at first-hand, either evidence of the phenomena or, on occasions, close encounters with it. The aforesaid Dr J Allen Hynek, in his own in-depth report, classified them into encounters of the first, second and third kind. The latter being visible contact with the little 'grey men' themselves. Dr Hynek's report was a book worth reading, where one could at least find much reliable evidence within its pages. When we mention facts and figures, around fifteen million Americans report what they perceived as unearthly craft, which is a formidable figure and cannot be ignored.

One would think that in this regard, the US population would have prepared itself for a final encounter or revelation of the facts by an actual appearance of the creatures supposedly responsible for it all, but that dilemma rests entirely with them. The aforementioned Condon Report could have gone some way in this preparation if it had not spent its energies exploring weak and largely unconvincing cases, which ought to have been disregarded in the first place.

Jacques Vallê, a serious investigator, was a well-respected French author who did approach the subject in a scientific way, more of whom we will mention later, with regard to his efforts. His comments on the above bulky Condon Report were that the conclusion of the Report was so packed with materiel that could only be described as irrelevant, made it possible that only the most determined reader could plough through it all.

Interestingly, a colleague of Jacques Vallê who was initially a sceptic, stated that he developed a sudden interest in the subject because, as he put it, "This book spent so much time attempting to dampen down the issue and convincing people that there was nothing to it and not worth pursuing," that he became convinced that there must be something to it.

No doubt, many others formed the same conclusion, which clearly indicated that the opposite effect occurred rather than that which was intended, but the entire phenomena did not just circulate around the general population, it reached the top so to speak involving a few US Presidents, namely, Eisenhower, Ronald Reagan, Jimmy Carter, and Bill Clinton. Since these men, naturally, in their capacity as a President, were also head of the Armed Forces and as such, would have to make important decisions on defence of the country. They would have, to some extent, rely on the advice of scientists and they certainly did so in the past worldly conflicts as also did Prime Ministers of the allied countries. We mentioned the branch of science involved in nuclear physics. They would obviously be aware of the universal makeup of matter and this includes everything on Earth and its occupants. Our entire body is made up of atoms, as would of course, apply to other worldly creatures and that the creation process that occurred on Earth, whichever way we choose to accept it, would also apply to creatures 'not of this Earth'.

Naturally, this could have occurred on other worlds much older than our own, so one would naturally expect creatures far more advanced than ourselves to exist in the vastness of space. If we have an expectancy that other world beings of a high order of advancement and intelligence do exist, this is belied by the fact that our process of searching for them has drawn a blank and nobody seems to be talking, of course, this does not mean that they are not listening.

However, one thing is for sure and that is, if our suspected little grey creatures are here, and have been for as long as the ET biological creation implies, then they certainly did not find us by listening but by far more advanced methods currently beyond our ken in order to get here.

A rather different panel of enlightened ones was convened that explored and analysed the possibility of contact with extra-terrestrial intelligent life. This was instigated by the Brookings Institute and their conclusions appeared in what became known as the 'Brooking Report'. This was initiated shortly after NASA was formed. Clearly, the final objective of NASA was to travel in space and eventually beyond our solar system, that we are approaching quite rapidly. The report issued dire warnings and predictions regarding what could be encountered when humans began to explore space. What is inferred basically was that it had to be considered that if we are going to open and peer into a mysterious box, then we must be very careful about what we may find therein; and, more importantly, its effect on the human psyche.

However, the whole point regarding the result of revealing the currently hidden and closely protected data is that no amount of hiding it away from the public will ever stop it from becoming known, eventually, and they must know this, also that by covering up and playing down, or denying the existence for the cover up in the first place, will only make things worse for the authorities responsible for all the secrecy and certainly worse for all the general population.

This only confirms, that the only logical and intelligent way is for a chosen body, either science or the Church to take on the responsibility of the gentle, gradual, preparation by a controlled release of all the data stressing the importance of the longevity of the phenomena's existence and therefore the most unlikely conclusion that it is a threat to humanity, but possibly, quite the contrary with respect to all that we might gain through such acceptance.

Mental preparations are the keywords, but surely, some will say, "ET must have considered all of these factors, yet still seem reticent to appear with full revelations." Because of our own ingrained behaviour patterns of conflict, war and aggression, we continually assume another intelligent lifeform would think and act the same and would covet our earthly resources for themselves. After all, they already seem to be doing so on our own Moon. Many books have been written on this topic, regarding ETs plundering the Moon for rare minerals when we referred to the whole phenomena of UFOs, the Greys and so forth reaching as far as Presidents, Bill Clinton seemed to portray an attitude (genuine or otherwise) of "What's it all about? If they do have alien bodies and extra-terrestrial vehicles hidden away, nobody has told me and I want to know."

Even Winston Churchill drafted a memo to a defence chief stating, "What's all this stuff about flying saucers? Let me know at your first convenience." The former Premier of Canada went even further and stated categorically that he knew that contact had been made with ETs. Would he make such a profound statement if there were no truth in it? We could also ask did somebody reveal this to him. If so, why not to US Presidents and Winston Churchill during his premiership?

The Canadian Premier would hardly make such an unusual statement 'off the top of his head'. Something of high importance must have been revealed to him and perhaps some of the others. Jimmy Carter however, was a different case; he was not going to wait to be informed and has even experienced a close encounter with the unexplainable himself. He was of the opinion that we certainly agree with today, that a full scientific enquiry and explanation of the phenomena should be undertaken, with a revelation of all that is currently known regarding alleged ETs and their technology (assuming they allow it). These proclamations had been made before and came to nothing, but Jimmy Carter made it clear that if he did become President, he would certainly make public all the factors surrounding the phenomena. One can only imagine how this sat with the 'faceless ones'. Here is someone who spells trouble. However, we would have asked, how would Jimmy Carter be able to reveal all the data if there was no one who would brief him when they had not briefed any of the others that went before him? However, once he had become president, there was a noticeable silence from the Whitehouse. Jimmy Carter, no doubt, soon began to realise that with regard to this subject that even being President he could not simply make demands like a latter-day Julius Caesar and be told all. He soon became noticeably quiet regarding the subject after that.

It certainly appears as though some power behind the scenes was dictating the policy of who had the 'need to know' or otherwise. In my book that I have titled 'High Strangeness' in the manuscript, I have suggested that there is a higher power behind the scenes that I refer to as 'the faceless ones', who possess security clearances far beyond Presidents and Prime Ministers (who after all are only short-term politicians). The aforesaid group comprises the mystics who have the power to decide who will be told, and what they should be told ... which amounts to practically nothing at the present time.

When we consider the huge amount of data that is retained (which is made obvious by the mass of deleted texts) in comparison to that which was released, it can only be logically deducted that the phenomena is real. Which brings us back to the fact that it will eventually have to come to light, but who will decide on this the Greys or the 'faceless ones'? Certainly not a politician. Of course, there are many scientists who do not worry or pre-occupy themselves with the issue and do not accept it in any case. Their views are valid simply because all the secrecy could only confirm to them that all this advanced technology they possess with regard to advanced flying machines and weaponry must be shrouded in secrecy at all costs. Also, they ask, show us just one tangible piece of evidence to confirm your belief in UFOs and their occupants. In this regard, another branch of science, medical science to be precise, may be able to do just that. A medical doctor or surgeon that is, by the name of Dr Roger Leir, informs us that as a specialist in dealing with traumatised victims of alleged abduction that have reached the stage of requiring to be X-rayed before possible surgery, have had strange objects, seemingly purposely inserted in various parts of their body. The objects show no sign of being rejected by the normal body defence mechanism, indicating the possibility that it was allowed for before insertion.

Dr Leir states that he has removed sixteen such items (which by now might be more). Naturally, these items were sent away for analysis with regard to their composition. They were said to be 'extra-terrestrial materiel. Before we read too much into this statement, we should add that it means their composition was similar to that of meteorites. One of the strange factors regarding these removal operations was that afterwards, the patients remarked that they felt somehow released. This would seem to indicate that certain alleged victims of the countless abduction claims were of special interest to the 'abductors'.

Another facet connected to this is that the beings we refer to as the

Greys have made it clear to the victims that they would easily find them again if they so wished. The subjects that had these inserts removed may no longer be found so easily. This would explain the reason that they felt such feelings as being 'released'.

When all this data is added to the abundance of evidence already supporting the E.T.H. or 'extra-terrestrial' hypothesis, it is hard to understand why some branches of science simply reject it all. This is hardly a scientific approach, and these are exactly the kind of people Dr J Allen Hynek was trying to reach out to. However, it is obviously down to each particular individual to evaluate the data and either accept or reject it. It has been suggested that our 'little grey visitors' not only have bases on, or in, the Earth but also within the Moon. For all we know, our Greys as well as being involved in our own origins, may also be the descendants of the creatures who 'engineered' the Moon and, according to Russian scientists, may have steered the Moon into its rather precise orbital location. We would imagine that our hypothetical Greys on earth are well acquainted with our current space activities. And, as our astronauts have made many sightings when accompanying their spacecraft to and from the Moon, they would have plenty of time to examine all the manmade artifacts that our astronauts have left there on the surface. These are artifacts such as the early Moon landers, excursion modules, take-off platforms, laser equipment and the Moon buggies. The Greys would therefore be well acquainted with the level of our technology, which, although sophisticated and advanced to us, to them, may seem quite primitive. A good example of this would be all the wasted portions of the Apollo craft, most of which end up discarded in space, and only a small capsule lands back in the sea.

Mostly, science would dearly love to become acquainted with the highly advanced technology of the ETs, but that would only happen if they all agreed on the sensible approach in order to gain it. Currently, this is far from what is apparent and we would assume that some of them must be involved in helping to produce equipment, that as one person put it, "Would send ET back from where he came from." Such thinking is a dangerous stumbling block in the way of any positive solution to this phenomenon. We have said that the entire phenomenon cries out for more intelligent, scientific, and government attention, but this does not seem to be forthcoming. When we mentioned the 'Condon Report', it was far from intensive, which is what one might have expected and was marred from the start by the employment of some members who were known as sceptics. That was fifty-five years ago and, in any case, the general feeling was that it carried more weight at the time than it really deserved, with regard to an in-depth enquiry.

Because of this, other countries whose populations were equally disturbed by the phenomenon were somewhat discouraged from setting up similar investigations. If countries of the size of the US could disregard it all so flippantly, then why should smaller countries get so upset about it and involve themselves in expensive investigations?

It does not seem to have any influential effect on the necessity for serious investigation, even after high placed individuals are personally involved in the situation caused by the phenomena. What better place for an intensive review of it to take place than the UN Security Council? In another chapter, we will highlight that two past directors of the UN Assembly were affected, one directly and the other indirectly involved with the phenomena themselves, but there are no signs that they instigated such a review.

Nevertheless, it turns out that in 1979 there was a suggestion, or a proposal, that an intensive enquiry into the phenomena should be carried out. It was a plea by the UN Outer Space Commission (how many of us even knew it existed?), to carry out a worldwide study on behalf of the UN into the subject. This, however, failed to germinate due to problems of serious lack of funding, so much for high interest.

If people wish for a certain thing to take place, they are told that we have to be prepared to pay for it, but are we not doing just that with our substantial tax payments, particularly those in the super tax bracket? However, another resolution, proposed about the same time 1979 in the State of Mississippi USA suggested strongly that a complete US Senate investigation of all the aspects of the phenomena be undertaken, but that resolution was defeated simply because it did not meet a legislation deadline, again, lack of interest. The same things happen in our own Parliament, where a debate is purposely continued until it is ready to be acted upon yet does not meet the deadline to be entered into the Statute Books. Politicians use various words to describe these 'ploys', such as 'filibusters' and so forth.

Considering the sheer volume of alleged UFO events and abduction claims in the US, it is surprising that there is such a lukewarm approach to the obvious necessity of such an enquiry. In Britain, our own authorities have not completely ignored the importance of the phenomena and around 1980, a serious debate of the issue was instigated by the House of Lords and one of its members, who was of the group that urged the debate was Lord Clancarty.

This member was also an author who wrote about subjects connected with the phenomena under the name of Brinsley Le Poer Trench. He also highlighted the fact that the sheer volume of sightings and landings was increasing all over the world at a noticeably alarming rate. This member in his books drew attention to the significance of the Northern Polar Regions with regard to UFOs that disappeared in the area, as though they descended into a base there.

He was not alone in his urging of a serious approach to the subject. Other members of the House of Lords added their weight in support of instigating a full 'in depth' study of the issue by the Government. They were such people as the Earl of Kimberly, Lord Davies of Leek and Lord Kings Norton, who was also a onetime Defence Chief as a Senior Admiral, all these gentlemen agreed that the UFO phenomena, especially the claims of alien abduction, could not be ignored, adding that it was of little use making light of the matter.

Science, it must be said, has the most difficult line to tread. Some scientists will not highlight themselves publicly if drawn to the subject of the UFO phenomena and abduction claims, in fear of damage to their reputation and standing, but others are quite happy to do so. Dr Stephen Greer, Dr David Jacobs, Dr Michael Salla, Dr Roger Leir and many others, possibly influenced by the encouragement of Dr J Allen Hynek.

It is strange in a sense, that any of the members of science would disregard such an important phenomenon when so many of their members, such as the astro-biologists, space scientists and of course, the whole NASA organisation are seriously involved in the process of training ET visitors themselves. That is, in the form of human ETs who may, long in to the future, encounter another world containing intelligent sentient beings themselves.

We seem destined to follow this process whether we want to or not, almost as though we were 'programmed' for it. Humans, in their strange unidentified craft, may be causing the same alarm among other worldly beings, perhaps similar to those people on Earth of 2000 years ago. If these other world beings looked up to some higher power and worshipped it, not being able to positively identify it, then humans would become their 'gods', of the skies.

When we consider the intensive signalling progress that has been occurring from the S.E.T.I Institution and the mariner space voyagers that have even left our solar system, containing all that information about us and our world that has been going on for decades, we would not, or should not be surprised if it was a recent phenomenon, but its sheer longevity, indicates, that the Greys in the shape of their forebears, have been with us for some considerable time and did not need to be invited, oddly, in the early days of the phenomena, it was fashionable to hear reports of golden hair 'Venusians' coming to Earth in order to investigate what we were up to with all those nuclear explosions, with dire warnings given to humanity. In another work, we dealt with the odd references in the old Hindu Texts, that seem to be depicting nuclear war thousands of years ago and backed up by the nuclear signature of melted brick and stonework and also fused green pottery shards, found at the location of what is assumed to be the ancient location of 'the cities of the plain' i.e. Sodom and Gomorrah. Therefore, the assumption that ETS were attracted here by these signals would be still valid, but instead of long golden-haired Venusians, they would be our archetypal Greys instead.

Of course, all of that would discount the theory held by many that the Greys predecessors were on Earth much earlier than that and were experimenting both with our (and primate) DNA and the end result was ourselves. It is no longer fashionable to bring up, as a barrier, the immense gulfs of space and how ETs could have crossed them, when our own sciences can come up with many theories how they could circumvent vast distances of space with the application of mathematics, suggesting wormholes, Einstein/Rosen Bridges, everything, but 'bee lining from A to B'.

In the story written by H.G. Wells, the Martians looked at the Earth with covetous eyes. Today, humans look at Mars in the same covetous way but not to conquer life, but to find some evidence of it, however small, past or present as previously said, it is what we are born for, to go there and even look beyond it. We are the ETs of times to come and may be repeating the future, the ET biogenetic theory of our own appearance, by carrying out the same processes on other developing creatures of another world.

If the same rapid pace of development and advancements from the Wright Brothers first flight to having a probe descending through the atmosphere of Jupiter, our great grandchildren may be capering about on Mars even some children being born today will see wonders to come and some will become astronauts, the process will never stop, intelligence breeds intelligence with no earthly restrictions. One of the major secrets of the human question, along with major creating powers, is the ability to understand and apply mathematics without which (just like every other creature) would restrict us to our earthly environment forever.

What a strange paradox when we consider that we are so close to conditioning Mars for our own life forms. When other humans are still blowing poison darts at their prey in some remote areas of the world and are still living pretty much in the Stone Age. This may well continue, if we stop chopping down all the trees and continue to advance into their domain, but our hypothetical 'grey entities' would be well aware of all the behaviour patterns of all earthly races, but may be bound by some cosmic laws that once successfully creating intelligence they must no longer interfere in their development, but of course, the alleged human abductions (depending on the object of the plan) would negate this. The Viking Landers on Mars are history now. The bouncing ball that housed the Lander was quite amazing. It did no damage to the craft and its sensing instruments that were inside and also landed with the outer shell opening up, with the Martian Rover in the correct attitude and not upside down, so it could easily roll out of the cocoon. That was in 2003, followed by curiosity in 2008 and now perseverance in 2021. Of course, other countries have reached the technical ability to send craft to Mars for various objectives of a scientific nature.

However, the initial Lander of 1976 was a stupendous achievement of forty-five years ago, but when we consider that the current objectives are looking for pretty much the same thing, signs of past or present microbial life, it must be quite frustrating for the astro-biologists when they have so many and varied projects they would like to be included, but the factors of expense, and the importance of weight factors have to be considered, so cannot all be included.

All these scientific experiments were considered as equally important, but some had to be eliminated. Obviously, the experiments that caused the most excitement with the Viking Lander would be repeated by more advanced methods, such as the early 'G.E.X' process or 'gas exchange' programmed. The Martian soil sample was subjected to a humidifying process and a large volume of oxygen was emitted when water vapour was applied to it. Naturally, this raised the hopes of the scientific team as NASA, particularly with its implications regarding the future terraforming plans.

However, as said, the main objective as well as trying to ascertain if things could grow there was the search for any bug that could produce evidence of their past existence on 'pre-catastrophe' Mars. Clearly, something quite profound occurred in the past that destroyed a living environment there. The results, although encouraging at first, seem to lose their significance later. When considering the possibility that the Greys could be quietly observing all of this with a certain amount of pride with the results of what their predecessors had achieved with the 'human project', we have to consider what their overall conclusions must be with regard to how the human entity is now characterised. One would expect that a planetary population of various nations that could live peacefully with each other and could settle any disputes in a civilised way by dialogue until a successful conclusion was reached could reasonably deserve the title of being civilised.

By this assessment, we can only conclude that the human entity must be categorised as uncivilised. Every day in some country around the globe, humans are murdering each other, sometimes dressing it up in terms such as 'campaigns', 'territorial disputes', 'defence' action and so forth, but the killing never stops. Nor does the rioting and wanton destruction, where people who enjoy violence and fire-raising for sheer enjoyment, and at the slightest pretext or excuse, hide behind legitimate protests. Who would facilitate this dangerous species being able to leave its earthly environment? Will this be tolerated? Would we tolerate it if we were in the position of our hypothetical Greys whose predecessors may be responsible for this most dangerous uncivilised yet scientifically advanced species by their efforts in the past?

All of our current advancements could have been achieved by our hypothetical Greys long before one of the experimental failures of their predecessors, that is, the Neanderthals, were sitting grunting around their campfires. If the Greys have indirectly inherited the responsibility for human kind, they could hardly just depart and leave such an uncivilised entity as the human to simply carry on with such negative behaviour. This clearly places a great responsibility on the shoulders of science, in particular medical science. They must utilise the intelligence that they have been given, and that has resulted in knowledge such as genetic manipulation to solve the mental and physical deficiencies, in order to bring human behaviour patterns in line with their scientific achievements and ambitions.

An equal amount, if not more, funding should be made available to genetic science to use the intelligence provided by 'God' (or the Greys) resulting in the Mars endeavours, to ensure humans are fit and ready 'mentally' to make the next giant leap for mankind. To return to the aforementioned Mars Lander experiment sniffing at the Martian soil in the Viking Mission, which was the gas exchange experiment, nitrogen was also released, along with the oxygen. We are aware that our atmosphere is composed of 78% nitrogen. Obviously, Mars appears to have all the essential gases that we have here on Earth, although not in the same proportions. Mars has predominately carbon dioxide. This eventually would be avidly devoured if we can get things to start to grow there.

One of the proposals suggested (among many others) was to purposefully bring about the melting of the Martian Poles, at which water is present along with the CO2 in the form of ice commonly known as 'dry ice'. This would invigorate the soil. There also exists, just below the Martian surface, a substantive layer of water ice.

All the earlier Martian orbiters and landers without doubt contributed greatly to the 'ground work' on which all the later rovers and landers will greatly improve upon. The curious thing about the earlier Viking experiments was that they appeared on the one hand, to raise our hopes in one minute, then dash them in the next. Most people will remember the geochemical analyses of a meteorite alleged to be originally part of Mars. This find, picked up in the polar wastes, when minutely analysed, caused great excitement at first. Then, a more cautious and reserved attitude prevailed toward this find. Many a scientist, no doubt with a sigh, muttered, "Here we go again." The significance of the analysis was that it appeared to show a microbiological lifeform, which is just what the quest is all about on Mars today. It took the form of a wormlike or caterpillar-shaped segmented form of life. The excited report flashed around the world 'extra-terrestrial life found,' but eventually this euphoria died down somewhat, due to various scientific after thought and certain remarks made. Initially, it seemed significant enough to encourage the US President, Bill Clinton, to appear on the television to announce it. Pictures of the tiny fossilised microbes were also shown around the world on all the TV networks.

If our 'little grey men' do exist, they could no doubt save a huge amount of expense and effort by our space scientists, but humans need to find out for themselves and learn as they go along and not have all the information they seek given to them on a plate. However, there is no doubt that more startling revelations may be coming our way and we must hope that no unnecessary influence or any kind of interference will be made by the 'faceless group' we have mentioned, which would put a block on any really profound discoveries made. The indications are that this would happen.

Our alleged 'grey visitors' may be well familiar with Mars, both on the surface and beneath it. We say this, because of the methane emissions being expelled from beneath the Martian surface, which seem to be regularly replenished. When we mention Bill Clinton's appearance on television with regard to the Martian meteorite, it was clearly spliced into an interesting sci-fi film (no doubt with full approval) titled 'Mission to Mars'. This film reflected on exactly what we are doing today, that is, the quest for Martian life signs. Another event that caused just as much excitement was the release of photographs taken by the early Martians orbiters of the so-called 'Cydonia area' on Mars, that seemed to show pyramid-like structures that caused the astro-biologists to remark 'they warrant a closer look'.

However, the most enigmatic photograph taken of the same area showed what clearly depicted a 'face', but if this seemed a step too far, the base did appear to have 'constructed' on very straight sides and the 'face' was said to be bilaterally symmetrical, but NASA showed later photographs which were said to prove it was coincidental 'trick of light' and shadow and so forth. The conspiracy theorists had a field day. However, the above-mentioned film did exactly what the astro-biologists stated and carried out 'a much closer look'.

Of course, the media are delighted with these revelations, particularly the press because even if the discoveries are down played or debunked later, they enjoy superb circulation figures beforehand. Naturally, all these events assist in the securing of further funding being maintained as they provide an air of expectancy as to what they may discover next. In this regard, we feel entitled to ask why a rover is not specifically assigned to go there and get up close and personal with the pyramidal structures, and even the 'face'.

Clearly, it would be a massive discovery if anything were discovered that showed signs of obvious construction, but again we must ask would the faceless ones step in again and take control of all the photographs and data. After all, if they can control Presidents with what they can or cannot reveal and blatantly defy the Freedom of Information Act, the problem of controlling NASA, an organisation that relies on government funding, would not present a big problem.

Even if a Mars rover, filming as it went, then stumbling on something quite profound, does not mean the public or the media would be immediately informed. There is a delay of the data to Earth, via the orbiter. It is not immediate and could easily be controlled during the time delay.

If we return to the supposed microbiological life signs alleged to be inside the Martian meteorite, it was stated as having lain there for thirteen thousand years. Naturally, the layman would immediately ask, how on earth could they know that? Furthermore, it would surely have been contaminated by earthly microbes or microorganisms. After all, we are told that there is nowhere on Earth, no matter how hostile the environment is, that micro-organisms cannot survive inside atom reactors, in boiling water, in deep sea geo-thermals, deeply frozen areas and so forth.

When reading of the deep analysis of such meteorites, we hear mention of nano bacteria. With regard to its minute size, some idea of this can be gauged when we are told that one nano metre is one millionth of a millimetre. Therefore, size is important (in both directions).

It is alleged Greys are well established on (or in) the Earth, also under the sea and in the polar regions, they would be well placed to observe (and on the Moon of course) all earthly operations of a scientific nature and in some aspects would be proud of our relentless quest for answers. But they would also hold a certain amount of pride in the accomplishments of their ancestors who we surmise are responsible for the more positive achievements of the human race, while at the same time being alarmed at what we are capable of when in negative mode. We have said, in another work, which is a little disconcerting, that since there must be an 'end game' with regard to their mission, how would it affect the continuance of ours?

A female abductee, when fully relaxed and sure that no harm would come to her during her alleged abduction, asked, "Why are you doing this?" The Grey, by way of reassuring her, stated, "Our operations are now drawing to a close." Of course, this could be interpreted in two different ways. Either they were talking about the operations concerning her abduction, or that they were referring to their complete plan.

We could assume that they meant the latter. After all, abductions have been alleged for decades. What more do they need to learn? It is for certain that the primary factor that would alarm them in the assumption that the 'ancient alien creators' theory is a fact, is that with regard to human crime, violence, rioting and warlike behaviour on most parts of the globe would be of serious concern to them and if their operations are 'drawing to a close', then what will be the final plan?

The most convincing abduction claim is the one we will be dealing with in the chapter 'Abductions and the Greys' which happened in 1961, that was sixty years ago, just how many people have been subjected to this trauma, and may have written it off as a dream long ago, but more importantly why so many? If 'they' were looking for signs of mental development, why not one abduction every five years or so? There is obviously more to the subject than the things we have considered.

It might seem therefore, that humankind could be on the verge of some quite profound revelations and whatever their content, they will almost certainly profoundly shock us. When one studies the Biblical events of a seemingly extra-terrestrial nature, many of which I have covered in my book Pillars of Fire, some appear in certain aspects similar to modern day abductions, but when analysed closely, together with the subjects and their earthly activity, they seem more like some kind of 'reward' for their earthly efforts and taken to (planet) heaven. When analysing these special beings who were known as the 'patriarchs', it is entirely possible that they could have been genetic creations installed on Earth to assist in the operations being controlled by the Greys who for fear of human reactions, did not wish to appear to the earthly population in person.

When scientists in general make what sound like factual pronouncement many people assume, most other scientists generally agree with them, but this is not always the case. For example, the science of palaeoanthropology, or in another case, our own Moon, how it got there, its makeup and the many odd aspects of it on which there are a very wide range of different views. There is no question, that the Moon is an enigma in its own rights with very little consensus with regard to its mysteries, but again, there is no doubt that our alleged 'grey entities' could enlighten us greatly on all the questions we could put to them, if it ever comes to that.

The Moon's orbit is so circular it seems almost as though it was positioned there, and a theory for this event does exist. I deal with many of the strange oddities of the Moon in my book When the Moon Came. If our alleged Greys can trace their earthly operations as far back as the appearance of the anatomically modern human (who many believe they had a hand in), then (in our terms) it would amount to some fifty thousand years. They could have achieved and been involved in many projects and operations with regard to planet Earth. Did the two Russian scientists get it right when they theorised that ETs 'hollowed out' the Moon and used it as a living environment steered by some unknown means into its current circular orbit? These two gentlemen were members of the Russian Academy of Sciences and were quite serious about their theory. Theories of any kind are quite flexible, they can be disregarded, reintroduced, modified and so forth. This would well apply to the theory that I introduced in When the Moon Came regarding the Moon being the original core of the planet that once existed between Mars and Jupiter.

The predecessors of our resident Greys could easily have landed on it, mined it out and adapted it to a liveable environment before locking up in earthly orbit. Many of these theories and assumptions sound like sheer science fiction, until we realise that our own exobiologists envisage exactly the same kind of operations themselves for our future astronauts to employ. They have suggested landing on an asteroid, manoeuvring it into earthly orbit and plundering its resources at leisure.

I believe that the theory I portrayed in When the Moon Came is as feasible as any other at the present time. Mark Twain's dry sense of humour is portrayed in many of the remarks he made and science did not escape his wit when he said, "The scientist will rarely show any enthusiasm for a theory that he did not propose himself."

When referring back to the lunar origins theory proposed by the Russian scientists, the strange thing is that all the lunar mysteries, except for how the circular orbit was achieved, were explainable when referring to their theory. The so-called 'Bodes Law' postulates where planets should be placed. And it seems to indicate that where the tumbling rubble we call the asteroid belt exists, there should be, or could once have been, a planet in orbit there. At some point in the past, there seems to have been a violent conflagration there – possibly between Mars and its once existing neighbour we could refer to as Planet X. With regard to the Moon, one of the main questions that science would like to ask of our alleged Greys is regarding the mystery of the lunar 'seas' or Maria. Liquid titanium and other refractory metals once flowed to produce the Maria. This is evident, due to the finding of some craters that had experienced this liquid material flowing over them and partially burying them. Material requiring huge temperatures to exist in liquid form. The obvious question would be where was the Moon passing in its travel, to incur immensely high temperatures? We can only surmise a close encounter with a sun (not necessarily ours). If such an event as the aforementioned conflagration did take place, the Mars would not have escaped scot-free. Imagine if our alleged Greys did reveal to us that a race of beings once existed on Mars and that now they have taken up residence inside that world and manufactured the correct amount of, and proportion of, all the gases they require and have learned to efficiently expel the methane emissions that all living things emit!

Our imagined Greys may have many amazing things to reveal to us; they may equal, or even surpass, the theory that they could have been responsible for our very origins. If we introduce the 'ooparts' or 'out-of-place-artifacts' that are obviously manufactured items from a technology of millions of years ago, it may indicate that humans as well as having reached a high technology may have been up to all kinds of mischief and negative activity that may well have brought about the flooding holocaust that seemed the only way to put an end to all the negative and dangerous activity. Speculation abounds when we consider how much knowledge of our past is hidden from us. It is difficult to imagine how (or if) we will ever know of it. If we swoop back to Mars for a moment and consider the methane that is being emitted, this could be a direct indication of inner Mars life forms deliberately expelling their unwanted gases in a controlled manner. This 'controlled' theory is based on the fact that the methane does not seem to be erratic, but rather appears to be continually replenished, indicating a regular volume being ejected. I am perfectly happy to have the theory I proposed in by book When the Moon Came rejected but only for valid reasons that would totally negate it. So far, we cannot disregard the aforementioned ooparts, but many members of science do so. The old adage "It can't be so it isn't" may apply here. The way in which the ooparts were discovered clearly indicates their extreme age.

The theory that I referred to above is that our Moon could have been the planetary core of a world that once orbited where the asteroid belt is now. I Offered a series of events that not only caused it to become Earth's satellite but seem to clear up many lunar mysteries along the way. If humankind has existed for many millions of years, it would change the whole pattern of the other theories that have been speculated upon. Certainly, the theories of the Greys being in our Earth space and that of alleged abductions would be thrown into confusion, simply because the evidence is so strong to support these theories.

However, the theory of intervention by the alleged forebears of the Greys in human evolution would be impossible to accept if anatomically modern humans were in existence millions of years ago. So one can see that whatever theory we align ourselves to, the ooparts cause a real problem and make it clear why science distances itself from them.

However, for all that, one day a valid reason to explain them must be found. If beings did once live on the surface of Mars, it would have been a very long time ago and most likely, other life forms must have existed alongside them and possibly taken below. The reason for this may have been a post-apocalyptic event between Mars and Planet X (now the asteroid belt). Science tells us that the Sun was at onetime thirty per cent cooler than today. The conditions and Mars, its neighbour, may have been very unfavourable when the forerunners of the Greys, the subterranean Martians and the inner Moon dwellers arrived long in the past.

As time passed, the inner Mars dwellers may well have travelled to and from Earth and many took up living within the Earth and the Moon. The evolution of the Greys may be ancient and some kind of reinvigoration may be underway, linked to the lengthy ongoing abduction plan.

All these possibly related entities may have originated in the star system 'Zeta Reticulae' and this possibility will be dealt with later. All this speculation will no doubt continue until the full picture and whole reason that the alleged Greys are amongst us finally emerges in some kind of final revelations yet to come.

A general feeling of expectancy is in the air and at some point a more severely enforced law and its strict compliance, will compel all and not just snippets of information will eventually have to be released, but the essential thing is, as we have said, that an intelligently compiled programme of gentle preparation should be implemented and not some kind of 'newsflash' or 'breaking news', with dramatic announcement issued from the TV.

When we mentioned a past conflagration that may have occurred in the region of Mars and the asteroid belt (Planet X) in 2007, a group of scientists undertook a study at The University of California at Berkley. This meeting was headed by a certain Taylor Perron. They calculated that the Martian poles tipped a full fifty degrees from their original position at some point in the past. All of this information came out in a recent television programme dealing with celestial mysteries, and these things don't just happen. We must consider the laws of 'cause and effect.' The same TV programme dealt with many of the mysteries that I covered in my book When the Moon Came. We cannot just refute or discount them, that is not (or should not) be the scientific way. It is quite an interesting, not the say, fantastic, proposition, that our alleged Greys could be so well entrenched in our solar system, but originated so far away. However, this would not preclude their compulsion to generate intelligence and full creativity by advanced genetic means.

Until the truth is revealed, free rein and conjecture will continue with regard to the issue and what is really so important that humankind, except for a select group, cannot be made aware of it? The mysteries of the Moon maybe just one part of a greater and more profound story, but it is surely better to speculate and 'assume' rather than coming up with a theory then preaching it as a 'dogma'. It may be dynamite in paper as the mathematical equations can be drawn up to support any theory.

However, the theory that the Moon came crashing into the Earth, then both globes obligingly recreated into the Earth and Moon, is a rather long stretch. Yet, some scientists will preach it as a fact rather than a theory. It seems that any theory will do it helps to avoid the difficulty of explaining the cosmic 'capture' theory.

If the collision theory occurred, it would make more sense if the combined rubble of the Earth and the Moon were just tumbling around the Sun rather like the asteroid belt. The late scientist Isaac Asimov stated, "By all known cosmic laws, the Moon should not be there." The abundance of retrieved Moon rocks was distributed around the world for the geochemists and certain scientific institutions to study. All agreed that the Moon was never part of the Earth. The astronauts of the Apollo programme brought back over 830lbs of moon rock gathered from different areas of the Moon and they differed greatly in their composition, actually causing more mysteries than providing any answers, and it is not surprising that NASA is planning to return there. And so, although Mars is top of their list in our human space objectives, primarily driven by our search for any signs of life and huge amounts of cash have been used up in the process, obviously the budget allows the Moon to be still not totally neglected, but the objectives will not be to further drill for microbiological signs and it is entirely possible that the actual mission profile is ultra secret.

For the lovers of conspiracy theories, most have concluded that the object of the mission will be a concerted effort to analyse, or we could say revisit, the many strange objects, glyphs and what seem to be markings, highlighting certain craters and even huge thin spires, not to mention all the flashes noted when orbiting the Moon plus of course the T.L.P of moving lights of varying colours.

The conspiracy theorists have it that something of very high importance has caused NASA to devote renewed attention to the Moon. Of course, in reality, a permanent Moon base there would require that water must be readily available rather than having to be ferried up from Earth and it is the discovery of this commodity from below the surface is the real motivation for regenerating the Moon base. Outbursts of water vapour have been noted. Using the Moon as a base for transmissions into space would be extremely effective with regard to the comparatively low wattage that would be required for transmission to great distances. With regard to the Mars missions, perseverance is a good choice of name when we consider that many missions and a lot of the spacecraft have ended in failure.

However, persevere, they did and now the results are plain to see. Once again, the conspiracy theories had an opportunity to link the aforesaid failures of the Martian missions to the actions of the alleged inner occupants that are very concerned about the plans of the earthlings to occupy and change the surface of their world.

It would seem, however, that the relentless force that is so active in the human with regard to the need to explore is irresistible and will always continue. As I write, history is being made with regard to Mars. The first flight of a man manmade helicopter (or drone) is taking place on Mars on this date April 19th 2021.

We have said that the mission profile of forty-five years ago is being repeated, but in a far more advanced and intensive way and much valuable information gained then is being utilised in the more hi-tech processes taking place today. To return to the fantastic achievements just accomplished, there is no doubt that it will progress to 'manned' helicopter flights, just as the Wright Brothers' first flight resulted in aircraft like the Concorde and the equally advanced military aircraft.

Many of the intriguing artifacts and what appear to be 'constructions' exist in rough terrain and these boulder-strewn areas would be difficult even for the cleverly designed Mars Rovers, but not, of course, for drones or helicopters.

When we covered the discovery of the Martian meteorite with what was initially thought to have shown microbiological life signs or a segmented fossil, which did appear quite convincing, it was not the only Martian meteorite that we found and minutely analysed, it appeared to show complex organic matter within its microscopic veins, on this, it is said, that the jury is still out.

It is almost as though some mystical force was providing all these items to arouse our interest in an almost tantalising manner, yet never allowing us to reach a firm conclusion to it all. When setting up the original Mars 'life search' missions, it is doubtful that the team expected to find any bugs, ants, or any small insects scurrying about. Those expectations were long discarded. It was simply due to the knowledge that tiny life forms on Earth can survive in the most hostile conditions and the 'tardigrades' are first class examples, and although the conditions on Mars are far from Earth like, it was a much more hopeful place to find such microbiological life than Mercury, Venus or the Moon.

It is of interest to note that a recent TV programme dealing with these matters, mentioned that science states that eighty-six per cent of earthly living things (mostly insects) remain undiscovered and also we know little about all the finer points of the mystical origins and beginnings of life on Earth with regard to our own species. Discoveries on Mars will no doubt raise many questions to be long puzzled over, just as we still do with the lunar rocks.

However, as we have said, the human brain is not a plodding instrument we can take on board and analyse many puzzles at the same time, just like a chess genius can march around all the tables in a chess game and make all the right moves and decisions against all the players. It is strange to relate that if everything comes to pass on Mars, future earthlings will look up at a blue sky with flying creatures introduced from Earth, see flowing water and oceans and live successfully on the surface, that if living entities live below the surface and have kept lengthy records regarding their ancestors, they would realise that history has repeated itself for them as well.

Our hypothetical grey entities on Earth would be well aware of all this and would also see that the instructions given out by their predecessors long ago - for humans to go-forth and multiply and till the Earth with the sweat of their brows - was not meant to apply only to Earth. Apart from the different gravitational effects on Mars, future living occupants whose origins began on Earth ought not to have their biorhythms disturbed too much with Mars having a similar rotation period and axial inclinations as the Earth, but the different gravity will have an effect.

Of course, future 'expat' earthlings on Mars will have no nice slivery orbs like our Moon to lighten up the night sky for them, just two odd potato shaped moons hurrying around Mars more like artificial satellites. One of these moons will have to be severely dealt with as if it is left alone it will eventually crash onto the Martian surface, but no doubt at that time the technology will exist to power it into a higher orbit or even on a course for the Sun to swallow it up. No doubt, the larger asteroid will be dealt with in this manner.

There seem to be some contradictions made in TV programmes of a scientific nature when dealing with the Earth/Moon relationship. One such statement was made that without the Moon, the Earth would wobble about quite erratically; surely, science in the main does not accept that? We see no signs of Venus or Mars without such a moon wobbling about. Some scientists seem so sure of themselves that they make certain pronouncements as though they are factual rather than conjecture. We are told that Mars has no magnetic field. The aforesaid conditions spoken of with regard to Mars, blue sky, birds and creatures, living on the surface etc., seems to ignore another scientific pronouncement that since our magnetic field diverts the solar wind away from the Earth and its dangerous radioactive breath, how will the new Martians be protected? The hypothetical beings living under the Martian surface may well be asking each other the same question, but the point is science tells us things that other members of their profession seem to preclude, that only leads to confusion among laymen. If the Martian atmosphere can be regenerated, then we would also be reinforcing the necessary atmospheric pressure and density to protect the planet Mars, just as it is protected from meteor strikes on Earth. But the same problem would still exist with regard to the asteroid and solar radiation.

With regard to any remarks made about the Moon being essential to the wellbeing of the Earth, we have to remember the many earthly legends from different sources that state at one period in the distant past, the Earth had no moon in the sky and speak of 'preselenes' or people who lived on Earth 'before the moon came', which I dealt with in one of my books dealing with these topics (When the Moon Came).

A strange situation exists with regard to the biorhythms we mentioned for people living on Mars. It was stated that when our astronauts spend long periods of time in orbit, then their biorhythms change to that which they would experience on Mars. This is surely a curious thing! This might suggest that if humans did exist millions of years ago, that it may not have been here on Earth. When we mentioned that the Greys could equally be existing inside of the Moon, they could, as said, be somewhat concerned about our plans to return to the Moon, particularly if the mission was to search for their existence, but cloaked with another explanation. On the other side of the coin, anything we do discover with regard to inner lunar or Martian occupants, these revelations may well be part of the agenda, with regard to what may be ultimately revealed to us at some point in the (perhaps) near future when our suspected Greys 'come in from the cold'. So they may not be all that concerned about our future plans and operations. When mentioning the alleged signs of occupation or evidence of any 'grey' entities that may be in residence in the Moon, they would surely at some point be evident on the surface when they felt it necessary perhaps with the surface structures being connected in some way to the inner workings.

With all the astronauts that capered about on the Moon, each of them, it is said, had a private medical channel with which to communicate directly to NASA via the flight surgeon. Only the astronaut and the receiving party would know of the message. There would have been nothing to stop them from reporting any issues of a non-medical nature.

If a message was in some way profound, the flight surgeon would have been able to pass it on to the appropriate section within the NASA organisation without even naming the astronaut (for his own protection). After all, the same fear among airline pilots with regard to any 'bogies' they encounter. They (if reporting them at all) put them down to 'air miss' reports. The astronaut would want to keep his job just as the airline pilot does.

Conspiracy theorists have declared that (with some substantiated evidence) that the Apollo 11 astronauts experienced an encounter with alleged extra-terrestrials and they say that there was a two-minute blackout during the comments to NASA by Neil Armstrong and that he was instructed to speak no further about it. Quite a lot of information could be relayed within a two- minute period. A certain TV programme dealing with Apollo 11 and the photos and comments dealt with in a session with Armstrong, Collins and Aldrin, showed close facial expressions and it was actually noticeable, that the three astronauts were rather downbeat and their expressions could be interpreted as guilt, shame, or even trauma. If, as some are convinced, the whole Moon landing was a hoax and filmed in Area 51, that would be a very good reason for their expressions to reflect shame or guilt. But another reason would be that they were still suffering from a certain amount of shock – especially after being told to keep silent about their encounters. One thing for certain is that if the whole mission happened as we are told it did, then their expressions should have reflected pride and joy with what they had achieved, and we should have seen their faces beaming with pride and elation. Yet, the opposite was clearly the case.

However, with regard to those who say the whole event was rigged never seem to ask Jodrell Bank who monitored the entire re-descent of the Lunar Module and even the part where Neil Armstrong had to steer the craft a little further past the designated landing area because of the dangerous boulder-strewn terrain there.

Some accounts made it clear to those receptive to any (even fake) news, that smacks of the unusual, stated that the astronauts did indeed register worry in their sombre expressions. Even Michael Collins, who did not actually stand on the Moon, looked equally glum. We must remember that he, more than any of the other two, would have more time to view, evaluate and register anything unusual seen on the Moon. The accounts referred to were picked up by 'radio hams' with quite expensive equipment and commented that they did report UFOs perched on the Moon and that their voice patterns were recorded and indicated shock in what they were relaying to NASA.

It is entirely possible that some gems of truth may exist within the numerous conspiracy theories, but the internet is awash with 'fake news' where certain people are flooding websites with such data and weave fantasies around a few true facts to produce their own stories. Although all this happened during the entire Apollo programme, the same will no doubt occur during the extensive activity going on with regard to Mars. Already a 'sphinx', another 'pyramid', a 'human skull', discs and all kinds of artifacts have been shown (but always from a distance).

One clear advantage the current rovers have is in regard to their ability to travel great distances with nuclear power sources rather than to rely on electric batteries of the more conventional type. Now we can look forward to many more surprises, but the conspiracy data will not abate and we will all have to be careful in our evaluation of the news and the reliability of the source.

Since the rovers can get up close and personal, why show those tantalising shots from a distance – such as the fossilised skull half buried in the sand, or the 'sphinx'? Simply get up as close as possible to them and closely photograph them or confirm them rather than just keeping people guessing. Since the objects have been shown and published on film, surely a mission is being planned to visit them in order to put an end to all the conjecture? As we have said, the same would apply to the Cydonia region, the 'face', and the pyramids.

The Mars rovers will be designed to cope with all the extremes of radiation (solar) high and low temperatures and so forth, particularly if they venture to the poles, where they would be subjected to temperatures of minus 120c, and with the high radiation from the solar wind will obviously cause problems during the lengthy process of attempting to convert Mars into a more comfortable environment. The radiation on Mars is said to be two hundred and fifty times the background dose we have to tolerate on

Earth.

If there are little grey entities under the Martian surface, they may well be concerned about human occupation, but would surely admire the human tenacity and determination to progress instead of giving up on the problems. Such beings, if they are the survivors of pre-catastrophe Mars, would have struggled and been just as tenacious with their challenges in making the inner zones habitable. Once their great work was completed, they would hardly have contemplated pursuing the goals that our Martian astronauts are going to face. If they had protection from solar radiation, protection from meteorites, even asteroids, protection from climate extremes and the fearsome dust storms, then why would they want to re-occupy the surface? Of course, if it was nicely terraformed, then maybe? Another minor problem is communication to and from the Earth, as mentioned. If we return to the Moon and set up the appropriate receivers and communication dishes, it would help matters. As it is, radio communications are said to take between four and twenty-two minutes depending on the orbital position of the Earth. And there would be similar problems with return communications.

Our own alleged Greys must have developed a highly advanced system of communication with their own world, which we assume is another solar system and obviously they could teach us much. The only problem with regard to highly advanced data that we could receive from them is the way humans would react given our still prevailing and negative behaviour on Earth. The human mindset would be the greatest obstacle. Lengthy conditioning by (we have suggested the Church) would be necessary to encourage humankind to sit and listen rather than harbouring negative thoughts such as world domination and the subduing of humanity. These are human qualities which we mentally possess and assume other creatures will also possess. Specialists on Earth wait with bated breath and being glued to their viewing screens will soon be clapping and cheering again, as each new revelation and discovery arises - to be sifted, analysed and logged into data banks relevant to the Martian plan. Some of this information is bound to be startling and quite profound and by manipulating the time in communication as was suggested with the Apollo 11. Revelations will almost certainly be retained for NASA evaluation before being released (if it ever would be), but, as said, this cover-up could not be maintained forever.

On a lighter note, if one of the Mars rovers suddenly encountered a little grey alien (or perhaps reddish) who popped his head up out of a crater to see what all the noise was about, clearly it would not become 'breaking news' on the television, but this illustrates the point that it will be the mobile rovers who will be the most likely human built artefact that will discover anything unusual.

However, as for the perseverance lander, one of the more interesting aspects of its choice of landing zone is what appears to be an ancient river delta and the presence of water in the past should be confirmed. As for the rest of the mission profile, we should not expect daily interesting communiques. Its main mission is to drill deep into various crater areas to gather up the dust, draw it into sterile tubes and seal them, then drop them into a box, rather like putting beer bottles in a crate. The box of samples is earmarked for deep analysis in an earthly laboratory. It will be collected by a very ambitious mission in less than a decade, designed to travel to Mars, collect the samples, and return them to Earth.

Another feature on Mars, little commented on, is that strangely some of the Martian craters are a little odd due to the fact that when viewing photographs from the orbiters, they in some cases are perfectly round, almost as though they were 'manufactured'. As far as we are aware, no one seems to have commented on this, but it would not seem natural for an irregular shaped chunk of rock, most certainly from the asteroid belt, to produce such a perfectly formed crater. The Martian moons themselves are a good example of this irregular shaped material as they are far from round. The Martian moons may have been blown into a course that would cause them to have encountered Mars and drawn into orbit about that world during the catastrophic period that may have involved the destruction of a world that is now the asteroid belt. However, when we consider the evaluation of the Moon rocks, unless the same uncertainty and mystery arises when deep analysis of the Martian samples takes place in our laboratories the question of past (or even present) microbiological life should be answered with regard to Mars.

If life of any kind does prove to have existed on Mars, one would imagine at first, that science would be staggered then of course delighted as indeed would include the rest of us, but it would be a major step forward from that revelation to find that life in the form of living entities exist right here on Earth, but are not native to it. There would be a far different reaction to that kind of revelation. Science, one would expect, would split into two camps, those of the 'let's learn all we can from them' and others, who would lend their expertise to the Government and the military factions, to look at ways of defending the Earth if these alleged Greys coveted the Earth for themselves, which of course is the human way and the fear of the unknown that is so deeply ingrained in the human mind.

They may see them as a dominating conquering force beguiling humanity with false promises that are really only hiding their own agenda, but even these type of scientists would also wish to know every aspect and detail of their origins, their evolution, their position in the galaxy, their cosmic capabilities and most of all any kind of relationship with humankind, but they may find it quite difficult to get the answers they require if they are shown to adopt an aggressive stance toward the alleged Greys, which in turn would cause the Greys to review their own contingency plans for the possibility of a violent reaction out of fear against an unknown foe. All of this, of course, reinforces the belief that the alleged Greys are working hand in hand behind the scenes with the chosen few that we suspect are keeping all the vital information from us because of this possible reaction from Governmental forces with scientific advisors, warning against alien domination.

Of course, other will say, this is precisely why these fully informed secretive individuals should, instead of secretly hiding vital information from Presidents and Prime Ministers and main stream science, fully inform them of the facts and that the alien technology are not intending to take over the world, but the fact remains that even the secretive ones could not know that for sure themselves. So there will always be a big question mark regarding the whole subject until such time as profound revelations are made.

This may be out of the hands of the alleged Greys. This major decision, after a thorough evaluation of all the data, would no doubt be made by the ruling body on their own world. We could reflect on just how much effect has been brought about, with regard to the 'self preparation' we have made in the production of a host of books, TV programmes and the film industry. The idea of intelligent advanced entities reaching Earth should have strongly 'conditioned' us to the possibility of it coming about and therefore made us consider how we ought to react to it, particularly as we have had so many 'signs'. Unfortunately, so many of the books and films have for the most part dealt with aggressive aliens ever since H G Wells (with a few exceptions) we have installed in ourselves the belief that any extra-terrestrial entities coming to Earth will always be of evil intent. So all in all, it has had no beneficial effect on the human mind set. Certainly a 'beneficial effect' in the short term, has been applied to the film industry who has amassed millions in box office takings from well produced sci-fi epics, but as regards to the audience going home, having a nightcap and going off to bed would be a far cry from what would happen if the film featured, came to pass in reality.

But for all that, nasty ETs blowing up all before them and scattering humans far and wide make for good entertainment, but we do not go home and have nightmares about them. Perhaps we should, when we consider what Tennyson said, "Maybe the wildest of dreams are, but the needful preludes of the truth."

It would be reasonable to assume that of these E.B.E's AKA our alleged 'little grey entities' are in our Earth's space, that they would have mixed feelings with regard to the 'human question' and may be glad that the final decision regarding their ultimate revelations or 'second coming' will not be made by them but rather their leaders on their own world.

One could imagine a discussion among ETs themselves. A certain viewpoint put forward might be, "Why let the humans carry on with all this wasted effort when we could reveal so much to them?" Another maybe "Nobody appeared to our own early life forms and presented a mass of knowledge to us. These humans must be able to progress by their own efforts and learn from their own mistakes. Unfortunately, they have not in fact learned from their mistakes with regard to violent activity. It was a mistake for this entire world to wage useless conflict, causing so many of them to die. Yet they made the same mistake again only a short time later. We are all aware that their science has lent itself to more serious activity than to improve their way of life. So much so that we have seen for ourselves how close they came to self-destruction by the power that their sciences discovered and consciously developed. It is therefore not surprising that these beings have been classified as a dangerous species by our cosmic laws, but the greatest dilemma for our own kind is the great responsibility imposed upon us by our own predecessors and their involvement in the very existence of these beings."

It could be a little disturbing to think that kind of dialogue could be occurring here on Earth. The possibility exists, but for all that, let us think positively. It has often been said (and the Greys would be well aware of it) that to invent, create, explore, peer into the depths of matter and our oceans also the vast expanse of the universe is what we are born (or created) for. But, advancement does not come cheap, therefore we must be thankful that those who sanction all finance for all branches of scientific research are far-sighted enough to provide it.

Of course, there will always be those who say that such finance should be diverted in order to cure all the social problems on Earth. Naturally, they have a point and these things are financed, although perhaps not to the extent that the socialists would like, but to stultify the progress of the far-seeing pursuits and adventures would tie us to Earth. It is not something we can prevent, humans are born to explore, and this does not only apply to our earthly environment, it is a force we cannot resist and we could say that the current achievements occurring on Mars are a perfect example of this. Everyone knows, or at least senses, that human activity will not stop there. Already probes and landers are being prepared to land or sink into the atmosphere of other worlds. Jupiter's moons may prove very interesting, in particular Europa.

When we mentioned the Greys with regard to all the data they could provide us with, it would be naturally quite extensive, since all the evidence implies that they have been in earth space for such a long period of time they would have thoroughly examined the other planets and moons of our solar system. Therefore, our missions and achievements, though quite stupendous to us, to them it would appear rather like 'baby's first steps'.

Apart from the Earth/Moon system, Mars is probably the most photographed world in the solar system and this, of course, greatly assisted the planners' ability to select a chosen landing site that may produce the most interesting data. In other words, we can now, to a certain extent, be somewhat 'picky' in the choices. Of course, the early Viking landers of the seventies were achievements enough by just landing successfully. At that time, the hope was that wherever a lander set down, as long as it had the necessary and sophisticated equipment onboard, it may find out all we needed to know about Mars wherever it landed.

However, as we have said, we can now be more selective; the gale crater as a choice is a very good one, given that it is considered to be an ancient lake and that there are signs that water once flowed into it. The information that provided this choice was, of course, brought about by the highly advanced photographic ability to produce high-resolution images. Whichever way we look at it, 'baby steps' or not, the achievements are notable. In particular, the successful flight of a helicopter or drone in such a thin atmosphere. This was not a 'let's see if it will work' operation. The mission's planners had already tested it in a vacuum chamber that was adjusted to be similar to the Martian atmosphere, so they were fairly confident it would be successful even in an atmosphere that is one hundred times thinner than on Earth.

When the serious analysis of the material in the gale crater begins, it will be looking for hydrated minerals or signs of past hydration and an announcement of such a confirmation would be highly significant. Another odd feature, but quite a dramatic one, is the canyon known as the 'Vallis Marinaras.' If it is possible to put a lander deep within this massive gorge, we will learn much (geologically) about the past history of Mars.

This massive divide is ten kilometres deep and dwarfs the Grand Canyon in the US in both its width and its length, but glaring dissimilarities do exist. The most obvious one is that with regard to the Grand Canyon in the US it has been cut down deeper and deeper by the force of flowing water. Indeed, a river still flows through it. Also, in the Grand Canyon, geologists can plainly see evidence of 'strata' that is, consecutive layers of deposits laid down over immense time periods of alluvial layers which can all be analysed in their turn, and produce much evidence and information about the past and any dramatic occurrences. In contrast, the great rift of Vallis Marineras shows little, if any, evidence of stratification; this immense valley seems in its appearance to have been wrenched apart by some massive but unknown force.

Science often tells us of the indications of past conditions on Mars, thicker atmosphere, water flow and wind erosion that would have been part of these conditions. Therefore, some evidence of strata ought to be apparent. Strangely, our own Moon, the great rift valley known as 'Hadley Ridge', that so amazed the astronauts for its beauty and grandeur, depicted an even more amazing sight which was the totally unexpected evidence of stratification. A process that seems incredible to have ever occurred on a world like the Moon, if indeed, it was stratification, as we know it, perhaps it was formed by a different process, periodical lava flows for example.

To be sure, it is far easier for us to imagine a deep mighty flowing river in this deep Martian feature than through the Moon's Hadley Ridge, which surely could never have had flowing water. We ought to be able to look forward to more amazing revelations along the way when concentrating on the main mission objectives of biological mineralogical and geological studies on Mars.

When we consider the anatomical advantages of the human, in particular, the enigmatic and highly developed brain in comparison to other earthly creatures. We may consider that all the achievements of a scientific nature that have been made were brought about by the use of only one third of the brain's cellular material, but we have said the excess must be there for some purpose.

If we return again to our hypothetical Greys in our earth space, they would no doubt be able to explain its existence which would bring us back to the eternal question "are they the beings (or at least their predecessors) who are responsible for the human brain in the first place and therefore equally responsible for our future?" However, some neurologists are of the opinion that much more of the brain's cellular material is used than we currently assume.

Although we are waiting with bated breath to be made aware of any discoveries made by the Mars rovers and any symbolic features that may be discovered on ancient rocks or edifices we have quite a number of them to explain here on Earth. we have said that it is no use raising people's interest when commenting on odd Martian features, observed from a distance, such as an alleged sphinx and other edifices, get as close as possible and either confirm or reject them. With regard to the earthly objects, many carvings, some that appear like a depiction of a galaxy and even symbols that seem to indicate the DNA double helix, go totally unexplained (or unexplainable).

These oddities are rather like voices from the past, but who were the 'carvers' and what are they trying to tell us? The strange thing is we cannot deal with them, solve them, then move onto the next case. We have many mysteries on Earth that still require an explanation, and not only on Earth but also with regard to our own Moon and now an abundance of them, which will no doubt appear during our Martian adventures.

With regard to the ancient earthly symbols, it is for sure that profound messages were being depicted in the best material possible for them to last. When we mentioned what could be interpreted as the DNA double helix, others appear to resemble the symbol of the 'god' of medicine with what appears to be the so-called 'caduceus' a rod intertwined with two serpents with wings depicted on it. A medical symbol that is still in use today and worn on the lapels of medical officers in the services.

Another commonly depicted worldwide symbol is the 'all-seeing eye' that seems to indicate wisdom and enquiry, which most humans seem to have been endowed with. It has been suggested that the symbol refers to a 'thalamus' that neurologists tell us is a central biological gland, with this name existing in the centre of the brain. It is said to act like an electronic receiver to deal with all our mental inputs. It is roughly egg-shaped and when this strange lump of organic material is sliced through, it resembles quite closely the Egyptian symbol often depicted said to be the 'eye of Horus'.

The (Asian) Indian culture often depicts the 'third eye' that is shown positioned in the centre of the forehead, that is perhaps signifying its central location in the brain. Perhaps we should pay more attention to the ancient symbols that seem to be attempting to tell us so much. Symbols are far more important than language. They do not need language, any culture could recognise them. It is the way that they are interpreted that is so important. Certain stories and legends interpret them as the work of an antediluvian group of survivors of the flood catastrophe even the survivors of the Ark of Noah, who with their long lives (as per Genesis) who travelled the world and left important data to be related to the survivors who would have been reduced to primitiveness. When they began to regenerate their culture, these symbols would be explained to them. Today however, our sciences are developing rapidly in medicine, genetics and so forth, but in the main, it is our cosmic adventures that seem to be the focal point of general human advancement.

With the advent of orbital satellites, that is the geophysical type who viewed the Earth from lower orbit and taught us so much from a different perspective. Again, in our alleged Greys would have done this long ago when humanity was in its infancy. Ancient charts that were copied from even more ancient maps have been interpreted by certain cartographers as having the appearance of being compiled from 'on high'.

Of course, we have the well-known Piri Reis map about which much has been written. Its salient feature is that it could only have been compiled when the Southern Pole was free of any ice. The Piri-Reis map is drawn accurately when it illustrates the Southern Polar regions. It shows every bay, cove, and inlet that is now covered in miles of ice. Surely a curious thing?

The earthly poles and the various expeditions there, particularly the South Pole, have instigated many of our current conspiracy theories about what is going on there. It is for certain that during the early Nazi regime they travelled all over the world looking for the roots of their allegedly ancient advanced culture or Aryan roots.

There is another ancient chart called The Orontius Finaeus Chart, which has also drawn many odd conclusions, one of which is that it could have only been compiled so accurately from a height of eighty miles above the Earth. How strange is that? Also, the Piri Reus Chart, when draped over a sphere, made more sense with regard to its compilation.

One of the odd things about the Southern Polar regions is that where the ice sheets are largely increasing noticeably in one particular area, it is melting in another. This, of course, could be interpreted as some kind of under surface heat source signifying underground secret operations or just simply a localised volcanic area of activity.

It has been stated that some strange unexplained activity is taking place in such areas as the McMurdo Research Station that is alleged to be highly classified. There exists an account of an aircraft on a medical rescue mission that flew over a large gaping 'hole', or what could be interpreted as some kind of entrance point. There was an air of silence with regard to this and after reporting it there was no reaction such as, "That sounds interesting," and an investigative team being sent out to survey it, but that did not happen. It was said that the flight crew received some dark warnings that they should forget all about it and must never fly over that particular route again or ever mention it again. It is not really surprising that so many conspiracy theories arise when the authorities behave in this manner. It would seem to indicate that the MIBs or Men in Black are operating all over the world. We are quite used to hearing about this kind of activity with regard to the UFO phenomena.

Furthermore, this kind of activity seems to reinforce the theory that our 'grey visitors' are working in secret with the faceless group that keep all the secret information to themselves. Such an alliance could have been in operation from a much earlier period than we think. For instance, before World War II an expedition to the South Pole gave rise to many alleged reports of a strange nature such as an account of highly advanced aerial craft that could fly rapidly from pole to pole. This, and other strange reports, were made by a certain Admiral Byrd who led a military expedition there using ships, aircraft, and balloons.

One of his strangest reports came from a balloon mission in the Northern Polar regions. He allegedly flew over the rim of an entrance that gradually descended into the Earth, and the temperature seemed to be increasing. The late Lord Clancarty, who wrote under the name of Brinsley- Le-Pour Trench, dealt with the adventures of Admiral Byrd and the various claims he made. If he was visited by the MIBs, it would not be veiled threats on his life but more of a character assassination, as even on his deathbed he was still speaking dreamingly about "those enchanted lands beyond Thule." The inference was that he was somehow mentally defective.

It seems strange in a sense when we consider the more high-profile members of the UFO groups, that is Dr J Allen Hynek, did not receive or at least admit that he had received a visit from the shady characters known as the 'men in black', but we must remember that he had once been an ally and had been involved in the hierarchy of the 'debunkers' in his early career and had worked at Wright Patterson Air Base. That is the place that has a 'foreign technology department' and the urologists make much of this, as 'foreign technology' would certainly include UFOs or parts of them.

The MIBs probably find it much easier to pursue more low-profile people such as the odd maverick journalist or outspoken ufologist who may be easier to intimidate and they have had some success in this. However, if we return to Mars and the human projects there, it is known that not far below the surface there are extensive water ice layers. One of the more exciting events is the rather convincing evidence of past and even present signs of water seeping onto the surface and producing gullies and channels on many areas of the Martian terrain, particularly noticeable on the downhill slopes.

This kind of activity may occur when such terrain is out of the glare and direct heat of the Sun, but there is no question that the signs are there and that there is little else that could cause these patterns, certainly not lava. The Mars global surveyor spacecraft was the orbiter that photographed these areas and it was stated that over a hundred different areas on Mars showed similar evidence in support of liquid erosion. These signs are not ancient but modern evidence, which is quite compelling, simply because when comparing photographs taken of the same area at different times, one can see changes with regard, for example, to the effects of running water. So these are quite recent events.

Of course, much of this sub-surface ice would not all be fresh water ice; it is often proposed or mentioned that Mars did once have ancient oceans and seas. Therefore, salt water ice below the surface would remain in liquid form more easily than fresh water ice with its high salt content. Unlike the Moon, except of course, the puzzling anomalies and questions that confronted the geochemists when analysing the Moon rocks, little else of interest arose when the Moon rover began travelling about. Of course, there are many oddities with regard to the Moon that arose due to all the Apollo missions. I have highlighted many of them in my book When the Moon Came, but Mars is quite a different proposition. It continues to throw up surprises and a lot of speculation.

If it is possible that other members of the alleged Greys that exist on our world are of the same stock as those that could be below the Moon or under the surface on Mars, producing all that methane being emitted there would be no shortage of water in their domain below the Martian surface. They would long ago have tapped and controlled the supplies seeping down through the crust.

We have to keep in mind of course that although the methane emissions could be due to a biological source, it could be from a wide range of life-forms and not necessarily living intelligent creatures, but there are far more indications to support that conclusion. Our Greys, for example, and the indications of ET activity on the Moon. The Russian space programme directors do not seem to silence their astronauts. The Russians encountered some strange things with regard to their early spacecraft missions to Mars. One of the spacecraft when photographing the Martian surface in the infrared, a rectangular pattern made up points of light or noticeable glows situated beneath the Martian surface. 'Rectangular' implies construction. This could be just one of the strange events that they have retained in their own keeping.

One could suppose that this would strengthen the case for any underground dwellers betraying their presence with the methane emissions. One of the groups that identified these emissions was let by a member of the NASA Goddard Space Flight Center. It was suggested that it was possible that other alternatives rather than ETs could be responsible for the methane, but this seems unlikely as it exists in such a volume that suggests that it is ETs that are responsible for it. It was also duly noted that future missions would have this item on their agenda to pay more attention to these phenomena, which science did admit took them by surprise.

On a previous mission to Mars, the Phoenix Lander touched down on an area near the Northern Polar Region, where water ice existed not far below the surface, and could be seen when the surface materiel was scraped away. As would be expected, the ice quickly melted away, but what was most intriguing was that when the results of the associated soil tests came in and all the various minerals in the sample were analysed, what it all seemed to add up to, was that this particular Martian soil had most of the constituents of basic garden soil.

However, as is usual, other voices prevailed. These voices basically said, "All this does not mean that future Martian colonists could start growing their spuds there." But we must keep in mind that future Martian occupants will have taken steps to enrich the atmosphere with oxygen and nitrogen, which would, of course, change things considerably. Nevertheless, some of the later experiments of the Phoenix Lander did seem to indicate a time in the past when Mars had high volumes of flowing water.

Of course, there will always be counter arguments and some negative responses, but the signature is clearly there with regard to water flows, but once accepting that factor, the situation becomes self-generating. As we have mentioned, to have water free flowing on the surface, other factors must be in play, temperature, pressure, and so forth. In other words, earth like conditions. All of this indicates the importance of being so selective on Mars, with regard to the areas chosen to land on and analyse. Naturally, budgetary expense is an important factor; we cannot send probes and landers everywhere.

However, there is a sense that some greater surprises may come our way when we consider the quite extensive areas of Mars already under analysis. All we have in order to make comparisons is our own Earth and its many different climatic regions. On Earth, it is difficult to find an area where life does not exist. On Mars, we search for areas where it may exist. From the frozen and barren wastes of the Polar Regions, to Death Valley in the US, we will find life, but when we consider that only one planet in our system is so conductive to life, it must cut down the odds enormously of finding a similar planet 'out there'. However, the possibility of inner planetary dwellers could be more widespread than we imagine it would make sound common sense in order to protect their species from celestial threats, which must exist elsewhere.

If there are underground living entities on Mars, they could not help but be aware of the surface activity going on there and, for all we know, they may be in complete communication with their counterparts on Earth, which is, of course the Greys. If this were so, they would not perceive their human visitors as a threat as they would be quite aware that all this human activity was due to the abilities of the human brain that had received the inputs or directives long ago to proceed in this manner.

The M.S.L or Mars science laboratory that was so successfully landed in the gale crater may well produce very positive results. Apparently, there were other choices that were put forward for the M.S.L to land at, or in. It was said that some five or other areas of choice were suggested.

Certainly, the area of the methane emissions would have been an interesting choice. The area concerned was named as the 'Nili Fossae' Region and was said to be the zone where plumes of methane emissions were noted. Perhaps this is one of the outlets where our hypothetical inner Mars dwellers are expelling their unwanted gases in a controlled manner. If the M.S.L was able to pick up and analyse these gases, it would reveal much, but it is possible that for full laboratory analysis it will have to be returned to Earth along with tubes of rock dust, but that would be some years away yet. However, no doubt, plans are afoot for this local analysis by a special mission; it would surely have equal footing in terms of importance, as that of the rocks analysis.

The data streaming in from the Mars missions will keep the analysers interested and busy for some time to come. However, returning to the Earth and the 'science and the greys' issue, we still have the situation to be resolved, with the UFOs and the alleged human abductions problem which must be resolved one way or the other. We have said that there must be an inevitable 'end game' or conclusion to it all.

Perhaps the Greys are waiting for an announcement rather like the exciting revelation of the Martian meteorite and its supposed microbiological lifeform that might come from the analysis continuing in the gale crater. If positive evidence of life, past or present, is found, the Greys may decide that this would be the time chosen to release the most profound revelation of all; where did we come from? The whole subject is becoming so well entrenched in what could be called modern day 'folklore' that the sooner the entire issue is resolved, the better. It could be said that science is so intensively focused on their operations with regard to where we are eventually going that they are losing sight of the still unanswered question of where we came from.

Solving the abduction issue with so many claims of a worldwide nature ought to be given a higher priority than it appears to have. Of course, although some dismiss it as a condition for the neurologists and medical branches to resolve, many scientists take the opposite view and have involved themselves deeply in an effort to verify it.

Whichever way it was revealed to us, confirmation that the Greys do actually exist would most certainly cause division in science. The acceptance of this as fact would be obvious across the board, but there would be division in the opinions on how science should respond. A substantial amount of scientists would have it in the back of their minds that this may be a type of dominating or occupational force. These scientists would only concentrate on the defence factors. It would be a similar situation to the Manhattan Project, when its scientists didn't know for sure whether the first nuclear detonation might cause a chain reaction and ignite the atmosphere. Or, it might echo the boffins in the C.E.R.N Project who are trying to create a black hole that might devour the Earth; they are intent on doing it whatever the consequences.

Many still possess the basic human qualities of suspicion. And so, suspecting ulterior motives, they may decide to conduct secret overnight meetings during which defensive measures would be planned. Humans are used to having (after centuries of it) the power to conquer, occupy, oversee, and control others over many centuries. It would require a massive mental readjustment from having the ability to organise and control in one moment, to being a subservient people in the next who would only exist as a result of an occupying force's 'kind' permission.

Another group of scientists would be clamouring to know so much that they would not know where to start with their questions. They might feel that it is their responsibility to think in terms of lending the specialist knowledge of the Greys to protect the planet and its people. Or, they may veer toward the military and try to utilise their knowledge of, for example, germ warfare. Unfortunately, there would be many people, such as in the top echelons of the military, who would be firmly fixed in the mental attitude of retaliation and defensive action.

Whichever way the revelation of ET life on Earth came about, there would bound to be a certain amount of cultural shock and social upheaval. But there would be absolutely no point in delaying something that is inevitable; we cannot begin to come to terms with it until it is known for sure to exist. The secretive ones, who are withholding all the vital information, are only hindering with their actions. They seem to be beyond the orders of the normal chain of command or countries' laws.

The well-known story of marauding Martians with killer intent, that stemmed from the pen of the late H G Wells and a couple of violent films about the story, obviously made an indelible impression on the average human. But strangely, although alleged ET craft have been spotted over all our vital utilities such as nuclear power stations, nuclear weapon storage centres, military air bases and so forth, there have been no sightings over facilities that specialise in germ warfare. These places seem to have held no interest for our UFO visitors. Or perhaps they don't know about them.

The obvious point is that the Greys would be far more advanced than ourselves, or else they simply would not be here. But it would nevertheless be wrong to assume that they are completely invulnerable. The antagonistic scientists might decide that the Greys' weakness, the 'chink in their armour', might be one of a biological nature. Perish the thought, but it just may be so.

Apart from the obvious questions that science would love to ask, such as "What do you want?" or, "Why are you here?" the kind of scientists we have just mentioned might never rid themselves of suspicion of the Greys. This is even more likely to be the case when the mindset of so many people has been moulded by years of threatening sci-fi films. A refreshing change to that kind of theme was a couple of films showing aliens with quite the opposite aims and intentions. It would be no bad thing if the more professional film producers dwelled more on this kind of approach - this would certainly help to change the human conception that ETs only mean earthly devastation and subjugation.

However, we are brought slowly to the conclusion that even if there is an 'end game', or 'second coming', along with final profound revelations that they must reveal, there would still only be the two aforementioned options open to us; acquiescence or retaliation. Most people must be aware that the first option is against the normal behaviour patterns of the human. As for the second option, this would be even worse for the human race. So, we seem to be in a 'no win' situation.

As all of this only reveals how humans with our current mindset are in the situation where we could be described as our own worst enemies. This is why we continually stress the importance of the right counselling and preparation by the physiologists and churchmen that we have mentioned. Some people will say (and it is a valid point) that we do not have to guess if it is all true. They point out that we are clearly told it is true by the actions of the faceless ones who deny us the facts by withholding, deleting, or not even recognising the existence of the documents at all. The bottom line seems to be, "There is a real issue, but we are not prepared to tell you at this point." Of course, there is an entirely different and more comfortable consideration for us to dwell on that would negate all the worry and stress that some people have put themselves through. Before mentioning this consideration, we would ask that all those who believe they have been abducted by 'little grey men' to leave the room. Now, we can consider this more comfortable scenario at leisure and without interruption. Suppose there are no UFOs, and no 'little grey aliens', and that all the bodies and craft that have been found are secret projects undertaken by humans? Suppose that disabled children (actually a real-life proposal) were utilised by the Japanese in secretive experiments. Suppose that they were seated inside a circular craft, and suspended from helicopters, in order to test the effects of loss of pressure and oxygen on the human body? Space medicine operations and testing still continued for a short time after the War. It would only require one crash, with the casualties strewn about the crash site, for the whole alien stories to begin. As for the rest of the crash retrievals, suppose they are simply advanced experimental craft (but not advanced enough to prevent them crashing all over the US). These would be the type of vehicles that the 'loose lipped' service man bragged about when he stated, "We have got stuff out there (Area 51) that are fifty years ahead of any other country." Now we can all relax (unless, of course, you are one of those people who is convinced that ETs did actually abduct you).

It is preferable to believe that it will be ourselves who will become the masters of the universe. And that it will be the 'ETs' of other worlds who will be pondering over, and watching, us coursing through their skies instead. Space travel has to start somewhere. Why not here on Earth? Think this way and you will all sleep better, until that is, someone stands up and says, "Do you realise that our current advancement only started around forty thousand years ago? That dinosaurs lasted for around one hundred and eighty million years? Do you really think that no other beings could have developed well past our own level by now on other worlds?" And the reply might be, "OK, you win; you seemed determined to bring us back to the same contemplative thoughts that keep some people awake at night."

Yet, on a more serious note, we do have a major issue that must be resolved either by a revelation given by our own human 'faceless ones' when they are good and ready, or by our little grey men themselves. After all, the latter, whether the secretive ones like it or not, do call the shots. One cannot help but wonder how long we will be allowed to go on developing and advancing ourselves, with our current space operations and long-term plans, particularly with regard to Mars.

From that eventual achievement to our actually visiting another star system would be a monumental leap, even if the objective was 'only' four and a half light years away, such as Proxima Centauri. Such thoughts themselves are light years away when we are still scratching around on Mars for evidence of life. We should, in logical terms, have spotted it all slithering, creeping, or hopping by as soon as the early Viking landers first started filming there. Especially when we consider the strange small creatures found on Earth that are named 'extremophiles'. More especially, the 'tardigrades' when we can see how they survive in the most hostile conditions. Bacteria can live on Earth inside nuclear reactors, in scalding water, in acidic environments, and even in liquid nitrogen at -196c. However, Earth, even in its extremes, is a totally different environment than Mars.

Yet, we have taken some of these microbes into space in experimental packages and they soon recovered their life functions on returning to Earth. Have any of the Mars landers ever taken any earthly microbes to Mars in order to observe if they could function there? Obviously, it would have to be in a controlled environmental experiment; we would not want them to mutate and cause a Martian-wide epidemic. But one might imagine that a Martian environment would seem far more comfortable than some of the conditions in which they survive on Earth.

We mentioned that science would ask the Greys for a description of their planetary environment, their planet's microbe's, its foliage and fauna, and whether or not the process of synthesisation occurs there. The common description of the Greys is not brought about by simple anthropomorphism; it is rather entirely due to the host of abduction victims allegedly describing their appearance in their hypnotherapy treatments. And they all recall getting a good view of them during the process.

With regard to Martian life, or life on any other planet in our solar system, we are told that a couple of billion years ago our Sun behaved in a different way than it does today. So how would this have affected the planetary conditions on worlds such as Venus, as well as Mars? How could we survive, or how did past life survive an increase of thirty per cent in the Sun's heat? Venus is the kind of environment that the purveyors of doom predict could happen on Earth if we continue to shovel all the carbon into our atmosphere. But nobody can ask the trees how they would cope with it. If so, they may reply, "Don't you worry about that. We'll take care of it."

With our relentless race to progress in all things cosmic, we may, sooner than we currently imagine, change Venus into a comfortable environment. The ways and means are already known to science. Venus is ripe for the 'terraforming' process, but Mars, of course, is our priority at the moment.

There are other oddities on Mars that have raised a few eyebrows. For example, the discovery of a large volume of Xenon 129, which science tells us is enough to display a 'nuclear weapons' signature. They make comparisons with the nuclear test sites that had so many detonations occurring before the Nuclear Test Ban Treaty was introduced. What is it doing on Mars? If this substance has a period of decay or a radioactive half life, then perhaps it could be calculated when the event that produced this took place.

One wonders what our alleged Greys would be able to tell us about that? When we speculated with regard to the conditions on their own world, they may have left it long ago. Especially if, as some ufologists suggest, they occupy the inner regions of the Earth, and Mars, and/or even the Moon. Perhaps it is they who manoeuvred our Moon into its orbit around the Earth, just as the two Russian scientists Mikhail Vasin and Alexander Shcherbakov suggested. If all of this did actually take place, then the theory based on our 'conditioning' by sci-fi films and books that the hypothetical alien Greys wish to conquer the Earth can be totally discounted (because they have already been here for so long).

There still exists a belief, even among those actively participating in the alien life search programmes, that because of the vast distances and immense gulfs that any alien visitors would have to cross, it is most unlikely that they could ever have reached Earth. This is a classical example of pure 'earthbound' thinking. Yet paradoxically, as we have said, they will often go on to refute their own misgivings by mentioning Einsteinian methods of easily circumventing these vast distances by mathematically possible alternative methods.

We have said that, if our 'little grey men' are here and have been for as long as is surmised by ufological and ancient astronaut theory, then an enormous amount of expenditure has been incurred by S.E.T.I and life search programmes for nothing. However, on the bright side, we could consider the huge leaps forward that our programmes could make (if human reaction allows it) with the help of the Greys. This would depend on whether our visitors assessed us as fit and ready to have this knowledge or not. And whether or not we were ready to travel beyond our solar system.

If alien life was shown to be true, where would the secret security people, and the scientists who must be working with them, fit in? Surely, their work would be over. Surely no one would wish them to be rewarded for their subterfuge and secrecy. At present, these people, who I have dealt with in my book High Strangeness, are currently quite indefinable and act above the law, with their refusal to comply with the 'Freedom of Information Act', which clearly means nothing to them. Mainstream scientists are in fact working with the top political leaders with regard to the general UFO phenomenon and attempting to get to the bottom of the reality, or otherwise, of the alleged abduction claims which a certain number of scientists are convinced is actually happening. To form this opinion, they must have necessarily worked closely with the abduction victims and assessed their character profiles and mental stability, etc. And these scientists are better qualified for the task than others who do not get involved but simply brush it off as nonsense.

However, even working out in the open and by appearing to be non-secretive, we still cannot guarantee that even in this situation we would be told everything. That would be down to political decisions after all the facts had been revealed to them. But at least at this point, the information would be in the hands of those who should be in possession of it all.

There is another aspect which is, if a profound revelations event did occur, we may all breathe a sigh of relief and explain, "Wow, thank goodness they did not tell us that." If a planet-threatening event was in process, and the Greys, working with science, managed to alleviate it in order to prevent panic and chaos, then that would be a good thing.

There are certain factors that would affect the decision of the hypothetical Greys with regard to their appearance and revelations. It would be their decision alone. But it would be the knowledge that we are continually closing in on the question of whether or not they are present in Earth space. This is due to the strenuous investigations by UFO research groups and also the ever-increasing numbers of scientists who are becoming more convinced that these phenomena (the abductions in particular) deserve closer and more united attention. This is largely due to the fact that the issue is long overdue for a resolution of it to be achieved.

When we mentioned the substantial amount of expenditure that might be saved if the alleged Greys did finally appear with a wish to kindly bestow upon us their extremely enlightened knowledge that we are seeking for ourselves. It would not call a halt to the expenditure in general, which would continue, but it may well have an arresting effect on the huge amount of cash disappearing into the 'black hole' of certain projects relative to defence. If humans allowed this, without panic or futile resistance out of pride, then it could, under the right circumstances, bring about world peace and stability. But perhaps we are expecting too much; an enormous readjustment would be required with regard to the current human 'mindset' of suspicion, aggression and all the ingrained behaviour patterns established in the human.

Such a hypothetical appearance of long suspected 'grey entities', particularly when we would be made aware that advanced and sophisticated as we thought we were, would all be shown to be wrong and we would quickly realise that we have a long way to go before being welcomed into the cosmic brotherhood, or deserve the title or being 'civilised'. A whole new attitude and mindset would have to be adopted. Many thoughts along these lines may have of course occurred to the alleged greys themselves and for all we know a final decision on a 'second coming' or revelations may be made on their world, which we referred to as 'planet heaven', during the Biblical escapades of the forerunners of our alleged Greys and just such a decision as was made two thousand years ago may well occur again and humans would be alleged to carry on as we are (until further notice). This would be better all round if it prevented such a 'cultural shock' as may occur until the human is more mentally prepared. Therefore, planet heaven may well issue the order, "Hold until further advised. There are signs they may soon cure themselves."

Now we can carry on in our own more comfortable way of finding everything out for ourselves. Just like many organisations, the funds for our usual enterprises, space activities, planetary research would not be unlimited, we would have to be selective in our choice of priorities for research. After all the research on Mars, if it did result in positive identification of past biological life or even active bugs still existing, then that may be seen as achievement enough for now.

However, this may not be the case. The Moons in our solar system have been proven to be very active and interesting and not just the frozen globes we once assumed them to be. This is particularly true with regard to the moons of Jupiter. They may have a lot of surprises in store for us. For example, if a probe were designed to descend slowly through the ice of Europa, a Jovian Moon, what would it encounter in the oceanic depths below? We seem compelled to search for life elsewhere, but is it really a different compulsion? A quest to find the secrets of our own origins?

Right from the beginning of human intelligence and self-awareness, we humans have always been somehow aware of a power greater than ourselves. This is perhaps strange in itself. Humans worldwide have credited their own existence to the 'gods' or to a singular 'god'. We have mentioned that humans have this strange unique individual identity, or what we have called a biological 'pin number', in the form of the fingerprints that are different in every person. And it is even more interesting to find that (as previously stated) when bodily decomposition occurs, the last tissue to decompose is that of the fingerprints. What possible force could be responsible for this? We hang on to our own individual identity as long as it is possible to do so.

The human is certainly a quite unique entity, and many more profound revelations may await us. The secrets of our own human origins still largely evade us. Dwelling on current evolution theories does not resolve the issue. We have much to learn. With regard to our hypothetical Greys, we could adopt two lines of thought, either they are just as curious and perplexed by our species, or they themselves had something to do with the appearance of humanity. This would help to explain why they might have been present on Earth for such a long period of time.

Over the decades, there has always been division on human views and opinions, and the same prevails with regard to the accepting or rejection of the UFO phenomena. There is division in politics, and in military thought, for example, in whether we need to accept nuclear weapons or obliterate them. This kind of division almost caused nuclear annihilation during the 'Cold War' between the Hawks and the Doves. There is also division in the area of religion; we have believers and non-believers, saints and sinners. It goes on and on.

Science does not escape it, as was found during the constant fight for funding by science with the main politicians. After Apollo 11, it was asked why more visits? We have been to the Moon, that funding could be better used elsewhere. We have mentioned in another work, the response of Jim Lovell, one of the astronauts on Apollo 13, "Imagine if, after Columbus discovered America, no one went back there."

Another aspect of the human advancement that is moving forward rapidly is the development of the artificial intelligence and robotics. We will soon be unable to detect an android humanoid from a real person. Even facial expression, the ability to blink, speak with an authentically sounding human voice have all been achieved. The ability to climb stairs and so forth has been proved possible and when all these factors come together in one unit, we will have duplicated almost everything in the human except two vital areas, the ability to reproduce and the possession of a 'soul'.

Yet for all that, compared to what our alleged Greys may be capable of, we may still be in our infancy. Over two thousand years ago, such entities in the form of what was accepted in those times as 'angels' who could even consume human food, were operating on Earth as emissaries of the Greys.

If humans were genetically 'created' by the predecessors of the Greys it was for specific and pre-designed purposes, one of which would be advanced creativity in order to carry on eventually the work of promoting intelligence and creativity far from Earth and in this we have already set out on the path to achieve that goal. Assuming the hypothetical Greys predecessors did create humanity; it seems to have been more orientated toward the development of the necessary genes to enhance communication abilities, creativity and higher intelligence, rather than to create entities whose body form metabolism would be adaptable to the biological changes and effects that would take place when we begin our space ventures. The human body is quite unprepared for space travel. Astronauts must exercise vigorously when outside the confines of Earth. The bodily rhythms change and it is said that growth hormones are affected.

However, it is entirely possible that our geneticists and biologists may be able to quite easily in the near future to 'modify' the body forms of future deep space astronauts to be able to travel comfortably in the environment. Everything travels back to the initial creation theory by alleged ETs. One view might be that once the highly advanced intelligent genes had been inserted, and were successfully manifesting themselves, then everything in its turn in a natural sequence would occur as required and the studies in space medicine that would have to occur as humans learned to fly higher and higher, eventually to reach outside the comfort zone of the Earth would all develop.

That foresaid intelligence allows us to confront, analyse and overcome every problem in its turn, and this is the process that is fully operational today. We could mention (almost) any subject, medicine for example, where the medical scientists speak of 'nanotechnology', where tiny devices could travel around inside the human body, locate, diagnose and even bring about the cure of any malady.

Another advancement (already in progress) would be in robotics, cyborgs, and artificial intelligence. The creation of entities that could function in almost any environment could travel with humans in the future to be utilised in any tasks that were necessary. For example, where vulnerable humans may be at risk. It is inevitable that special units that are 'bio-engineered' for deep space journeys will be developed.

One of the most important factors in human development that needs to occur is a remedy for the many problematic features. These problems, such as mental degradation, mental illness, Alzheimer's and dementia, horrific criminal tendencies, and of course the tendency to destroy each other in war, have no place in such an organ that has been 'gifted' to humanity. They must be completely eliminated by any means possible - and this may necessitate gene manipulation.

It is puzzling in itself how these problems came to exist in the first place. We have said in other work that they may represent failures in the work of our assumed 'creators'. This is easy enough to imagine with regard to hypothetical ET 'creators', but with regard to a divine infallible creator.

The bottom line, is that if our suspected Greys are with us, they may have the ability to correct their forebear's mistakes quite easily, but most probably find it less problematical to allow humans with the intelligent genes already installed to solve all these problems themselves. We can only imagine how humans would react if the Greys did appear in their 'second coming' and began to instruct all the clinics, prisons and hospitals to send their patients and inmates to have their brains adjusted at designated venues.

If, before instigating such a plan, they made it clear that they could cure all forms of mental and physical illness, then humanity may be more willing to comply. The most positive factor that points toward the reality of the UFO phenomena and in particular the alleged human abductions, is the very fact that so much information in regard to the topic is withheld from us deliberately by an untouchable group who seem to have power over and above an elected Government and laws passed by them.

We can only hope that science has come up with a plan or course of action in order to deal with what must inevitably happen with regard to a final 'end game'. Anything but a military option. The scientists of the secretive group would have to meet with mainstream science, the latter being informed and brought up to speed with regard to all the previous information withheld from them. Such a hypothetical plan would have to be drawn up under the contingency requirements. It may be a long time before it may be implemented, given the possibility of a situation we mentioned before, where the Greys' planetary hierarchy may have introduced another postponement.

The scientists among the secretive group are certainly doing a very good job in terms of secrecy when we consider that many among the 'unenlightened' ones still question the whole validity of any Greys existing on Earth at all. Or any abductions taking place. In the meantime, we simply get on with the procedures we seem almost 'programmed' to complete on Mars - the orbiters mapping the surface of Mars and the landers sniffing, drilling, and scratching at the Martian soil. If the Greys do exist and are working with the secretive group, they will be simply getting on with their own agenda while the secret agents and their scientific counterparts will be busily adopting all the advanced technology that has been given to them in exchange for their own plans, while the Greys carry on with their own operations, which by now would have involved very close contact with humans.

Nevertheless, mainstream science is doing its level best to uncover the mystery of whether we are alone or not, both in the Martian adventures and in the continuing S.E.T.I programme. However, it does not look, at the moment, that anything in our own solar system will answer the questions we seek, although it could happen anytime on Mars (if we were told about it). And as said, we still have many experiments and plans with regard to the many moons in our solar system.

A book, whose title reads, We are Not Alone and states that extraterrestrial life has been found, is misleading because the contents of the book do not prove this. The book is very interesting if you are a biologist, a chemist, a geochemist or a mineralogist, but is heavy going for the layman to understand. However, it would certainly help to bring awareness of all the effort, expense and the success of the Mars orbiters and landers at the time of its publication in 2010. As a university course book, it would be invaluable.

Since that time, further landings and missions to Mars have occurred and in the best locations that may produce the best results in our search for life. As previously mentioned, good news could come in at any time to justify all the effort and expense. Plus, of course, other countries also have their Mars missions and exploration plans. Nevertheless, the arguments still exist and are quite valid, that the expenditure would serve a more noble purpose if it was devoted to the social services and their requirements, as we have said. But the fact is, humans are born to explore. There is little we can do about it and it cannot be restrained. The social problems requiring financial attention get it anyway, albeit not at the rate that many would like. Naturally, if we accept the theory that advanced 'other world' beings are responsible for our current cosmic exploration goals by giving us the intellect to do so, and the ability to master advanced mathematics (without which we could not do so), then among many other things, the many earthly social problems may be overcome once the human behaviour patterns had been overcome and modified. Then, a huge amount of cash would be saved running prisons and mental homes etc. Ideas we may never have considered or thought about may suddenly be made to us. If this is the ideal situation and certainly one would prefer, then this makes it even more mysterious why the secretive ones, instead of keeping information from us at all costs, would surely be working toward the opposite aim and preparing humanity for such better things to come if we act accordingly.

One view is that the assumed 'end game' is taking so long to come about because the Greys have some fear around how humans would react;

some of our emotions and behaviours are quite predicable. Also, 'they' would be well aware of how thin the veneer of civilisation is with regard to humans, which has displayed itself so often in violence.

After the hypothetical postponement of their first chance to appear to humanity - which was even prophesied by the emissary Jesus in the form of the second coming (making clear to whom Christians have been praying) - it is now being postponed again. Two thousand years ago, it seems that humans were more ready for such a revelation, even expected it. They may have needed to make some mental adjustments with regard to the higher power, but that is all. By contrast, these days, humans have made huge advances in technology and weaponry, but they are still the same belligerent beings that they were at that time. And so now, the problem for the alleged Greys has increased immensely. No one knows how we would actually react. But it would almost certainly not be in the way that the people of Biblical times did; at that time, it was more in line with falling on their faces in awe rather than falling over each other to attack them.

If the Greys could pull off such a second coming without incident, another revelation might be that we here on Earth are the only other intelligent lifeform in their known galactic travels. Obviously, this would be quite a shock, but it would not retard our space activity. Instead, it could serve to refocus it with regard to our future objectives. The Greys may let us know that no other species they have found in the galaxy has been worth the effort of working on to enhance their intelligence and creativity. These species may not have been suitable for such a project simply because they had no suitable prerequisites to improve on, such as bipedal possibility, or manipulative digits ideal for creating things.

All of this, of course, would make us continue our programme towards terraforming, populating, and spreading our life forms throughout the galaxy as we were originally instructed to do when being ordered to "Go forth and multiply."

But why have we had absolutely no response, or found any kind of signalling evidence from anywhere in space? This has caused people to ask, "If the universe is supposedly teeming with life, where is everyone?" Aka the 'Fermi paradox'. As a result of the (supposed) lack of signals from space, people have become complacent. So, if this was all suddenly turned on its head by a sudden revelation that the Greys are among us, this would indeed be traumatic. Of course, a lot of thinking beforehand would have gone on by the Greys and by our own scientists and all the religious groups of the world. The latter are the ones who would experience the least trauma because they have had hints about all this in their ancient writings. And they should therefore be the group that handles the prelude to it. The main problem for the Greys, of course, would be the reaction by humans, and the question of whether or not their presence on Earth would be accepted.

It is interesting to conjecture that at some point in the future, if humans do take on 'the burden of creation', whether we ourselves may be in the position of facing major decisions with regard to a possible success in our own plan. How would we go about the process of revelations with regard to any intelligently enhanced beings we may have been responsible for? We may have infused intelligent creative genes into a suitable recipient, who, as per the plan, may have developed at a speed far ahead of any other species on their planet, just as has happened in our own evolution over the last forty thousand years. We cannot guarantee that any future intelligent creations brought about by human hands would develop at the same rate as ourselves. But when we consider the amazing scientific activities being carried out by the ancient Egyptians, who had by then had thirty-six thousand years to develop, they developed to a remarkable peak of achievement. This amount of time is a blink of an eye when considering cosmic scales, or even in terms of primate evolution.

In my book The Modern Ancients, I write about how the Egyptians had progressed to performing medical operations and carrying out advanced dental bridgework that was comparable to modern-day medical achievements. When we consider these things, it reflects the absolute uniqueness of the human brain and the rapid mental advancements it has made in comparison to so many other living entities on our planet.

Over one hundred and eighty million years, other species that possibly existed on other worlds could have evolved and expired many times over. Huge cosmic events could have brought their existences to an end multiple times over. We wonder, if such events had not occurred, would those creatures still be around? In only a tiny fraction of that time, the humanoids appeared and expired. Homo Erectus appeared and expired, and the Neanderthals appeared and expired. Where did this sudden 'force' come from? The force that seemed to be busily experimenting to eventually produce the human entity once the hapless creatures that had lumbered about the Earth for so long were conveniently removed?

Everything to do with the human entity produces nothing but questions and wonderment that many do not even question. So many just proceed along a path of existence and take our human unexplained abilities for granted. But there is no doubt that eventually, surely some major event will occur that will explain all the oddities.

With regard to the major question of the Greys and their possible connection with human history and their lengthy interactions with humanity for so many centuries, it is most certainly a subject that demands an explanation equal to that of the human question. The whole subject causes nothing but division among humanity. The division in human evolutionary theory, the divisions in the subject of the entire UFO phenomena, division about the alleged abductions and the Greys.

All of this makes it seem inevitable that some kind of profound revelations must occur. But the biggest problem that we must ask is, "how will humans handle it"? The answer to this question may well affect the decision on whether it will happen at all. This major decision may not be in human hands in any case. Until such time, we will remain as divided as ever in our opinions.

Many people do not think about it all, or at least do not dwell on it. It is comfortable to accept divine creation and avoid thinking about awkward questions. It is acceptable to many that our ancestors were apes. Some find this more palatable than the idea that we stem from a highly advanced creative force 'not of this Earth', but secretly believe that humans are vastly more ancient than most people care to imagine. This idea is indicated by the mysterious ancient artefacts that we call 'ooparts', that have been found from millions of years ago. These ooparts are the work of humans - such as buildings and monuments indicating sophisticated construction - but are from far further back in time than our traditional ideas on how long humans have been on earth. So, therefore, many use this evidence to point away from ancient astronauts as the cause of our advanced intelligence, and point instead to ancient humans.

However, science tells us that long ago, the Sun was thirty per cent cooler than it is today. Therefore, the planet Venus could have been quite suitable for human habitation. Then, over the Millennia, when the Sun's heat began increasing, Venus may have become a roasting hot greenhouse and more difficult for habitation. This sounds similar to what is happening on Earth today. History does repeat itself, it seems.

When this occurred on Venus, we began to make plans to scamper off to Earth. First, however, we may have wanted to rid Earth of its undesirable occupants, and so perhaps we simply chose a suitably large asteroid to get the job done. If the Sun was thirty per cent cooler in the past, then it has increased by 30 per cent. How would we cope with another substantial increase? Would this be the time that we move to Mars, having prepared it for our arrival?

Eventually, we will have to depart much further afield when our sun loses control of itself. But at the rate of scientific progress in things cosmological we should be well prepared for it. At this point, all those scientists who preferred to take the view that we are the first sentient intelligent beings in the galaxy will be able to adopt the 'told you so' attitude and feel quite pleased.

But today, we are still left with the problem of our 'little grey men' and we cannot refute the signs of their presence. Whatever we say does not rule out the aforementioned possibility of human activity in the past, although it may rule out the possibility of ET genetic creation. Indisputably, the revelation of the existence of Greys, along with their actual appearance, would be a most profound event and would affect the Church, the sciences, but most of all, the people. The latter will be the worst affected. Having said this, we have no evidence that people all over the world were fainting when Copernicus stated that the world was round. After all, the ancient Greeks stated that many centuries before him. It is a fact, however, that certain ladies did, in fact, faint during a conference spelling out and dealing with the Darwinian theory of evolution. All was fine until the moment that revealed that people were once monkeys. We can only imagine how such people would react to the aforementioned scenario of an ET appearance. The military would be the worst to be affected. All the petty conflagrations all over the world would seem irrelevant and pointless and any aggression by the military in the US, where we could assume the 'second coming' could occur, would be almost impossible unless they chose to adopt the horrifying alternative option mentioned in my book The Second Coming. The military would be rendered impotent and would have no role to play.

Science would fare better than all the other sections of society. They would be the most interested and would be falling over each other for all the advanced information they could possibly attain. As for the Church, as we have said, they were already expecting a 'second coming' anyway, and so they would accept it as such. They would only have to adjust their expectations with regard to golden winged angels. The Church would not witness a situation where the righteous were separated out from the wicked, but no doubt the wicked would be dealt with in ways we could only imagine. Medical science may one day, with some assistance from the Greys, help to advance a procedure whereby humans would be treated like a car in a garage with a diagnostic plug inserted in order to identify the faulty circuit and rectify it.

Probes attached to the skull, and the neurosurgeons working with the geneticists, would quickly identify any faulty circuit. The geneticist would then go about the business of snipping out the faulty gene, or group of genes, and the patient would soon return to the ranks of the normal.

All of this, of course, could happen in time with no help at all from our hypothetical Greys. But they would nevertheless be aware of our progress, and it would be bound to affect when they decide to appear to us. On the other side of the argument, their appearance might save humanity many years of patient research and study. Perhaps they have a sense of responsibility to make it clear to us directly, without leaving it to the faceless ones, the true fact of our origins.

But it is disturbing to think that scientists in the mould of 'Dr Strangelove' are outside the loop of the secretive ones that are allegedly working with the Greys. This separate group may only think in terms of defence (along with the military) of the world and think only in terms of belligerent action to free the world by taking a course of action involving biological means developed supposedly for 'germ warfare' operations. Yet, there must be many level-headed scientists and senior political figures who have thought long and hard over the issue and developed plans and scenarios on how to handle any conceivable situation. Recently, an interesting TV programme dealing with the ancient astronaut topics, stated that a previous Canadian Defence Minister named as Paul Hellyer, spoke of the so-called 'Federation of Nine' who are the nine 'principles' or (we could say), the key players and that our alleged 'little grey men' are a member. Many will say that this is due to the many sci-fi movies and conspiracy programmes on the television, and this having a psychological effect on certain humans. But to some extent, NASA counteracts this dismissal by issuing many seemingly corroborating explanations. The fact is that many people distrust NASA and believe that they are holding back much evidence that would only strengthen the beliefs of many in the reality of the ET phenomenon. NASA will quote ice particles, cosmic rays striking the eyeballs of the astronauts, misidentification of discarded parts of the spacecraft that were shed during the launch (even though they could not be seen at the time). They will state other reasons such as space junk, satellites, and optical illusions - anything to avoid any more shocking truths.

Some of the astronauts must be quite offended by this, but they are subject to the same attitude that prevails in civil aviation. Filing an 'air miss report' is fine. But if they elaborate on their sightings, perhaps veering toward the unexplainable, then their jobs may be in jeopardy. This is probably no less true with regard to astronauts.

The explanation of 'optical illusions' is not exactly new. It was suggested to Galileo over four hundred years ago when he published his discovery of the four satellites of Jupiter that he had observed and noted in his 'Sidereus Nuncius' in 1610. The scholars of the day refused to accept his findings and offered the aforementioned explanation. But he at least escaped with his life.

It is quite amazing that such an explanation could be offered when trained observers, such as pilots and astronauts, make what they feel are reliable reports. And there is little they can do about it. So they live with it. But 'optical illusion' is a rather weak explanation, not to say offensive, when applied to very qualified observers.

When taking the whole phenomena, including the alleged human abductions, we cannot make light of it. It is a serious issue, but many would not wish to mentally accept it. The author, Arthur Koestler, in his book Les Somnambules attributed this kind of attitude as 'psychological purblindness'. He wrote that this arises from a great fear of accepting what could entail an enormous change in our outlook and values and thereby deciding that it would be far more comfortable to mentally suppress it.

It is strange but noticeable that this contrast in attitude and beliefs still exists in scientific circles. The UFO expert, J Allen Hynek, came up against this situation himself when working with the military and the scientific communities. When we mentioned the enormous period of time that the dinosaurs existed on Earth, and if an E.L.E event had not put paid to them, they may have lasted even longer. The author M Pierre Guérin states, "The speed of evolution of the species need not be exactly the same on every suitable planet, it is entirely possible that our mental state of development (and of course, the sciences) may well have been passed on numerous worlds in the cosmos." On our world, two examples of this occurred - the lightning fast development of the human mental evolution as seen in the ancient cultural evolution, and the development of the sciences and technology from Wilbur Wright's take-off, to Neil Armstrong's lunar landing - all in a person's single lifetime.

But with regard to our still unresolved but very important issue of the UFO phenomenon, even when the issue was at its peak during the 'project blue book' and the Condon Report, much merciless 'pruning' of unexplained sightings took place. These were whittled down to just a few that were reluctantly classified as 'unexplained'. All of this negativity toward a problem that requires intensive research may have had the opposite effect upon the masses to that which was intended - and it may come back to haunt them at some point in the future.

All the efforts to play down the obvious seriousness of the issue are doing nothing by way of preparing the public in a gradual manner, or slowly making them evaluate how they should react when having to soon face the possibility of its reality. Wilbur Wright and his brother's first manned flight apparently took place in the very area now occupied by the Wright Patterson Air Base. The Foreign Technology Department is said to be where parts of machines from foreign sources are analysed. What could be more foreign that parts of alleged UFO crashes?

However, the area most favoured for this kind of activity was the infamous 'Area 51'. Its very existence was denied for decades, but now the authorities have finally openly admitted to its existence. All the interest and long-range photographing, and people attempting to get closer and closer despite the 'deadly force' warnings asking trespassers to keep clear, has meant that some now say it has been relocated to another nearby desert area.

For science and the authorities to still refute the existence of the UFO phenomena and the possible existence of the Greys certainly requires the denial of an enormous amount of issues. The additional factor is the apparent longevity of the phenomenon, even reaching back to Biblical times. This indicates centuries (in our time) to the present day. People in high positions have also had 'close encounters.' Many of the abduction claims entail 'alien' inserts in the victims' bodies that are said to be made up of materiel that is contained in meteorites. Incredible stories told by the alleged abduction victims in hypnotic regression sessions seem unbelievable, but do, in fact, run to a pattern.

We must also add all the sightings made by the astronauts and that have allegedly been reported by them and photographed when travelling to and from the Moon and orbiting it. They have reported 'glyphs', items that look like altars with some kind of 'symbols' on them, and items described as some kind of spires or what we might call 'needles', as seen in Egypt. These have said to have been some fifteen stories high. Some have assumed that they are some kind of communication devices or 'ariels'. Such devices might seem to be quite primitive for such alleged advanced creatures. Structures have also been noted, given code names, and reported as the astronauts passed over them.

With regard to the alleged 'structures', they are just one of the items that the debunkers often seize upon, by explaining them as 'pareidolia'. Pareidolia is the name given to when the human brain attempts to bring symmetry and order to chaos. This can occur in such places as Monument Valley in the US, or the Giant Causeway in Northern Island as a few examples.

The aforementioned Area 51 is inexorably linked to the UFO phenomenon ever since the controversial 'Roswell Incident'. Some retired Area 51 personnel have been interviewed and admitted that very advanced experiments have long been going on there, and that any questionable craft (whether they are earthly or not) are not simply wheeled into the hanger after flight tests, but are lowered into underground locations. Some ex-employees have responded to probing questions as to what is going on there. The reply has been, 'you name it and they are studying it.' It has been said that levitation and anti-gravity experiments, and all kinds of scientific projects, are being studied in underground locations.

Of course, there are no restrains in speculation and conspiracy theories, but there would be no reason for these ex-employees to be lying. Only one ex-employee, named Bob Lazar, has come out and plainly said, "Yes, experiments are occurring with extra-terrestrial craft." But they are likely bound by secrecy as a contract of their employment.

All the speculation will continue until such time as the 'secretive ones', who openly fail to comply with the law of the land regarding the Freedom of Information Act, decide to reveal the data that they are withholding. Or, until the Greys themselves decide otherwise. Releasing reams of documents with the text mostly obliterated is not complying with the law but simply saying, "We know the full facts but you do not need to know them."

These mysterious figures are not impressed by rank or position or any high-profile people, even presidents who rather lamely state, "I tried to find out but came up against a brick wall," (presumably of silence). This is not only recently, even as long ago as the time of Winston Churchill, he made it clear that he wanted to know "What is all the business about flying saucers all about? Your urgent reply would be appreciated." As far as we know, his secretary made light of it, probably because he did not know any factual data himself.

Even during the Battle of Britain, Air Chief Marshall Hugh Dowding believed whole-heartedly in life existing on other worlds. He virtually stopped Adolph Hitler in his tracks and made him suffer his first defeat (presumably with no help from the Greys). Many of his pilots in action reported 'hostilities' or 'bogies', but one presumes none of a circular design passing at enormous velocities. Even the late Duke of Edinburgh was most interested in the phenomena and wondered why the issue still remained unresolved.

President Truman, in his turn, voiced his concern as he was in power when the whole phenomena was regenerated in 1947, with the well-known 'Roswell Incident'. He was said to have formed the original group of scientists, military leaders and so forth that were said to be called the 'Majestic 12'. However, at least they were well-known people who operated openly and were apparently above board.

Today, nobody knows who their modern-day counterparts are, but even back in the days of the alleged 'Majestic 12', they all had to be seen as 'singing from the same song sheet', or else they were in serious trouble, if any member broke the silence. Later, we will discuss a 'whistle blower' who suffered fatal consequences of doing just that.

Although nobody knows the identity of the silent ones, it is clear that they have great powers of immunity. A certain Dr Stephen Greer, who seems to have great experience in these matters and could well be putting his safety at risk with regard to some of his pronouncements, tells us that he has spent around eight years probing into the cone of silence with regard to the UFO phenomena and all the secrecy and has urged all this time, that the US Government exercise the power it has at its disposal to resolve the issue. This would only be possible if the information was released in accordance with the Freedom of Information Laws. A noticeable paradox is that huge sums of cash have been sanctioned for so-called 'black projects' that even high echelon politicians may not be made aware of, due to their low security rating. They may even be unknowingly helping finance the actions of the faceless ones during their operations with the Greys in some mutual deal. We hope that they get something in return for their finances behind the scenes.

The late Dr Carl Sagan made a noticeable change in his attitude from speaking openly about alien life and the possibility that ET could be here. He was busy working with S.E.T.I and producing messages on gold discs, even telling possible ETs who may encounter the voyager craft leaving our solar system, then suddenly seemed to change course in his attitude and veered more toward the ranks of the 'debunkers'.

More high-profile figures of other countries have mentioned their concerns that the issue continues to go unresolved. One time premier of the USSR Mikhail Gorbachov was among them and made it clear that the whole subject must be treated seriously and not as amusing conjecture. The aforementioned Dr Greer is in possession of masses of valid documents showing clearly that there is much subterfuge with regard to the existence of alien craft and their occupants. Also, the reality of the so-called 'Roswell Incident' has official documents popping up from time to time, indicating its reality.

Hoover, (J Edgar) did not like his organisation, the FBI being left out of the loop with regard to that issue and in certain documents made reference to a crashed disc and alien causalities stated, "We wanted information on it and to see it but the army grabbed it and wouldn't let us see it." With regard to the massive amount of finance that is diverted into highly classified 'black projects' which have to be approved by US politicians, when they may not be fully aware of what the cash has been used for. Dr Greer stated that it amounts to around eight thousand dollars for every man woman and child in the USA with regard to the comments we made to the late Dr Carl Sagan, in a recent TV programme Dr Greer revealed that Dr Sagan was furtively approached by some shady individuals who gave certain 'advice' to him that seemed to cause his transition. Also, we have an ex-president when asked about the UFO and the abduction phenomena (Bill Clinton) had said, "No one has told me and I want to know," that he also was approached and 'advised' in like manner.

With all that Dr Greer is revealing, it would not be surprising if Dr Greer himself has not, or will not be visited as others have. It was also noticeable that another ex-president, that is Jimmy Carter, went suddenly rather quiet on this issue when formerly stating what he would do about it when gaining office (as we formerly mentioned).

The list of presidents and other high profile political leaders is quite long, who, after speaking out on the issue, did not choose to utilise the power that they had to do anything positive about it. We could also add another past President, Gerald Ford, to the list. Astoundingly Dr Greer remarked that he had information to the fact that a certain ex-president was informed that he, Could end up like Kennedy if he pushed it too far.

This is not to infer that Kennedy was assassinated for that reason, but just to reiterate that the faceless ones had the power to do so. The 'licence to kill' syndrome was not only a feature of James Bond films in the past; it is still alive and well today. Many high-profile figures have added their voices to the fact that UFOs are real. Many pilots have not publicly reported them, but as for the reality, when the Chief of The Federal Aviation Authority says they are factual, then we ought to listen. He obviously would have seen in his capacity as airlines supremo, many reports from pilots from all over the US, who had reported encounters with unidentified aerial craft and that they were not of the usual type, encountered in air miss reports. This did not mean, of course, that they were not secret US projects, but their flight patterns and manoeuvres made this difficult to believe.

It is mandatory by law that airline pilots do report near miss encounters or violations of aviation procedures, but the pilots are reticent to refer to them as UFOs which of course, they are, but it is the implications of the term 'UFO' that they fear. Other aircraft can suddenly appear on the same flight level, causing dangerous close encounters, possibly due to the faulty altimeters or wrong air traffic information; aircraft fly at different flight levels to avoid such encounters.

However, with regard to the phenomena in general, the ufologists and the conspiracy theorists show convincing films of alleged beings resembling what we have come to know as the Greys, being sliced open on the operating table and state that some qualified surgeons have remarked that nothing in the procedure clearly indicates fakery. Yet others state that horror film companies could easily produce such material on film with the special effects procedures they have at their disposal. When we spoke of people in high places urging that all the secrecy be lifted, we could add the former UK head of the Defence Forces, Admiral Hill Norton, and his US equivalent and one time CIA Chief, Admiral Roscoe Hillenkoeter. His name appeared on the list of the often-mentioned 'majestic twelve'.

However, any majestic twelve that exists today would not have their names clearly listed, as was the case after the 'Roswell Incident' and President Truman's involvement in the issue. It was once stated that 'power corrupts and absolute power corrupts absolutely.' However, we would not suggest that this mysterious cartel that obviously exists today is corrupt, but they certainly seem to possess absolute power.

Although it has become noticeable that more and more PhDs and so forth are joining the ranks of those who know that there is something rather profound and important that needs to be faced up to and finally confronted, there are still many in the scientific community that distance themselves from it, they have become known as the scientific 'theocracy'.

We briefly referred to the 'licence to kill' syndrome that certainly seemed to be alive in the past, and may or may not still prevail. We formerly referred to the onetime Defence Secretary, James Forrestal. He wanted the whole truth about the entire UFO phenomena and the presence of ETs (the Greys) to be told to the public. He argued that it was pointless to keep it hidden when it would have to be revealed in time, in any case. Forrestal died under suspicious circumstances; he was found dead below the window of an institution that he was being treated in. Maurice J. Jessup, as well as others, also died in questionable circumstances.

These are only assumptions put together by the conspiracy theorists. Nevertheless, it was inferred that these extreme measures were also sanctioned in cases where the economy could be seriously disrupted by the use of certain inventions that would, for example, provide free and cheap energy for the masses which would negatively affect certain sectors' profits and losses. A cartel of powerful industrialists could quite easily engineer an accident with regard to the inventor. When we mentioned Stephen Greer and his revelations, he touched on the case of Nicolas Tesla, who envisaged cheap and plentiful power for all in order to help the less well-off masses to improve their lives. Tesla was an electrical wizard, but his proposals made him an enemy among certain industrialists. Tesla was found dead in his hotel room; it was alleged that the FBI opened the hotel safe and took away all his files, data, and records.

He clearly must have felt threatened and concerned that this may happen or else he would not have put his data in a secure place. Who is to say whether this sort of practice does not, or could, not occur today, especially if the economy was threatened by the loss of billions of dollars of technology that could become widespread and obtained cheaply?

The average man on the street has no conception of what is going on in the background or behind the scenes. Even the Queen herself advised such to Mr Paul Burrell who, as butler to Lady Diane, was accused and arrested of theft when he took her personal belongings away for safekeeping. The situation arose that could not have been tolerated – one in which the Queen herself might have been brought to court as a witness. Clearly Burrell must have told her beforehand. The Queen allegedly told Burrell that 'dark forces' were behind the scenes who could be dangerous.

This was the kind of thing that came out in the tabloids when reporting on Burrell's trial and eventual exoneration. However, the term 'fake news' may be recent, but the activity is not. So, we have to ask, how would the 'dark forces' react to the possibility of a single individual releasing information that would startle and disturb the entire population of the world? These forces may see only two options – discredit or destroy.

The US Government certainly cannot be unaware that there is a greater power at work at a higher echelon than that of the main seat in the Whitehouse Oval Office. The alleged Greys may be quite happy to have this 'stalemate' of secrecy prevail, as long as it suits them and allows them to continue with their programme undisturbed. They may decide that they will deal with any future scenarios when the time comes and when it suits their purpose. In the meantime, let the 'dark forces' maintain the present 'status quo'.

When the US Senator by the name of Barry Goldwater, who was also a retired high-ranking officer in the US Air Force, approached his friend General Curtis-Le-May who was head of the Strategic Air Command and asked to be allowed to visit him at Wright Patterson Air Force Base, all went well until he asked Le-May if he could see the so-called 'blue room' that he had heard of, Le- May was furious with Goldwater, "Don't ask me that again, even I cannot go, so you certainly cannot go there." The 'blue room' was alleged to be the place where all the ultra-secret items and information were stored, possibly even bodies.

Curtis-Le-May was a man who could blow up half of the world in a nuclear holocaust, yet could not even possess the right security level to enter a certain area on his base. What chance would a President, who after all is only a politician holdings a high office for just a couple of years, have to attain such a level of security clearance? Yet he was the head of the most powerful country in the world! Dr Stephen Greer mentioned a certain Boyd bushman who was near death and like some others in this situation who felt that they had no longer to fear reprisals, spoke of allegedly true facts regarding the Roswell incident and what was going on in Area 51, and so forth. Boyd Bushmen related that at one point, when he was working at Lockheed Martin (the commonly named 'skunk works') that he was supplied with pieces of UFO craft distributed among himself and other top engineers in order to 'back engineer' them, no doubt to be able to understand how the UFO worked. This would inevitably lead to constructing a complete craft and then flight-testing it, as is alleged by Area 51 'watchers'.

The parts that Bushman was presented with were said to be part of the antigravity equipment that the alleged ETs use and his task was to study and develop on it. this would seem to indicate that the crash retrievers that are reported so often are completed craft that are not quite understood in the function and retrieved by the secret operatives to wherever they are flight tested from.

There is a strange paradox here, among two separate conspiracy theories. If, as we suspect, a selected group with the highest security classification, are working with the alleged Greys for highly advanced technology and giving them a free hand with their own agenda, in which the abductions seem to feature highly in, then why would the group that are said to be doing all this 'back engineering' having to struggle to figure out all the technical data with regard to the functioning of the ET craft it would seem that the Greys would simply supply them with all the data they need. One explanation is the 'back engineers', are outside the loop.

So, the only answer can be, that the security classification of those places like Wright Patterson Air Base and certain departments of Lockheed Martin and so forth are far lower than the top echelon group working with #the greys' who are separate from Area 51 and that these are the secretive ones denying any information that was ordered to be released by law and get away with it.

With this policy of releasing various pieces of alleged UFOs to various highly skilled people to study and analyse over a wide area, the individuals are reporting on the function of each portion, would not be able to envisage the entire craft or even know if it was alien, but simply captured 'foreign technology'.

However, there is an interesting comparison here to a passage from my book Pillars of Fire, where I related the story of Solomon and Sheba and their offspring 'Menelek'. Solomon adored his son and said, "What can I give you that is not ordinary," Menelek asked for the Ark of the Covenant at rest in Solomon's temple, they came up with a plan that artificers in all the crafts around the city would copy each individual piece, but would not know the function of the whole or its appearance.

We have said that with all the alleged crash retrievals of UFOs going on all over the US are almost certainly manmade. Indeed, if the Greys are actually with us, they would not be too pleased with 'earthlings' having the view that they could travel the galaxy yet fall out of the sky all over the Earth.

The whole story of a crashed alien craft and its retrieval may all be entirely based on a single event, the Roswell incident. It is extremely unlikely that a team geared up and ready with transport facilities and a group of military looking individuals displaying no identifiable insignia, would be able to get on the scene so quickly if they were not prepared and put on standby when an advanced experimental aircraft was about to be flight-tested in their area. Naturally, the public, when witnessing all this secretive activity, warning them to back away and keep silent about what they had witnessed, would almost always assume it was an alien vehicle. With regard to the starting point of it all, that is the 1947 event, a certain US Air Force Officer named as Philip J Corso, clearly stated that the noticeable burst of high technology that occurred and accelerated over the next decade up to the onset of the Space Programme was due to the study and development of alien technology.

The sudden appearance of Hi-Tech items and technology is undeniable, but no serving officer would reveal such data and openly defy the Official Secrets Act with such impunity. This would apply across the ranks from a private, to a general, and would be continue to be enforced even after retirement. So there is obviously some ulterior motive behind this occurrence.

It may well have been part of a diversionary process or so-called 'Black Propaganda' issue. In any case, most, if not all, of the firsthand witnesses have now passed away. However, as said, the 'sudden burst' of advanced technology was quite noticeable fluorescent lighting, special alloys and metals integrated circuit (microchips), fibre optics, laser technology, even domestic items in the kitchen reflected it, Teflon, non-stick frying pans, Kevlar carbon fibre components, a very lengthy list of items 'suddenly' appearing including fibre optics even materials that were essential to the later shuttle programme such as the heat resistant pads that were fitted to the areas of the craft presented to the atmosphere on re-entry.

So much data has been presented, written about, denied, confirmed, exaggerated, and certified as genuine by (now deceased) persons. So much has become speculative that it may never be proven one way or the other. Unless, as said, during some final 'revelations' occur, which all of this always comes back to. Nevertheless, the highlights of the event are worth mentioning. The 509th Bomber Group in 1947 was the most technically advanced squadron in the US Army Air Corps at that time. Since most of its Officers and enlisted men were carefully selected, it would not reflect favourably on the group if its Senior Security Officer by the name of Major Jesse Marcel, could not recognise a simple weather balloon (even it if was a more advanced type) that all the people in the area were quite used to observing.

This outfit had actually delivered a couple of atomic bombs on Japanese cities. Clearly, this Officer (Marcel) was a scapegoat and deliberately told to hold pieces of a real weather balloon while being photographed and subjected later to ridicule. It is said that if it is in the interest of high security, character assassinations were sanctioned and even real events, as we have hypothesised, applied to humans such as James Forrestral and Maurice K Jessop.

If the 'balloon' explanation was the highly secret 'project mogul', that would explain the secrecy and the military recovering every single scrap of it. The fact is, it was still a balloon. Furthermore, it has been stated by the UFO logistics that the study of downgraded documents shows that on that particular day there was no record of such a release. So, argument and counterargument will always prevail. The mogul project was designated to listen out for other countries' nuclear tests, particularly the Soviet Union, and it would have had additional special equipment, but at that time there was no other feasible explanation for the strange material. The balloon theory is rather weak in comparison to the so-called indestructible items found and tested in such a voluminous amount, where crates of the stuff were shipped back to the air base referred to as 'higher headquarters.'

Major Marcel himself had collected some of the material and was convinced of its 'unworldly' qualities. But the bottom line is, if a general says to a major, "This is what you say," then it is what he would say. The odd thing is, when analysing the train of events regarding this material, it was so strong that it resisted all the severe tests applied to it to try to destroy it. We must ask how could it have been blown to pieces so easily by a lightning strike littering the ranch that belonged to Mac Brazel, who brought some of it into town to the sheriff's office? It was stated that he remarked that his sheep would avoid it at all costs. In addition, that Brazel himself was quietly pressured to say no more about it. The strength of the threat may be indicated by the fact that he did as he was told. In addition, it was said that he was seen shortly after driving a brand-new pickup truck.

We have mentioned that J Edgar Hoover Head of the FBI only became aware of it three years later and complained in an official document or memo shown by those who obtained certain downgraded material later. He was clearly out of the loop, as he was known as a 'volatile' personality. This particular year (1950) was a noticeably active time of UFO activity. Even the current Head of the Catholic Church, Pope Pius XII had a close encounter in the Vatican gardens. I cover this particular event in the chapter 'The Church and the Greys'. It made quite an impression on him.

In 1950, it is doubtful that the Churches outlook was as broad-minded as it is today with regard to the UFO phenomena and with what it implies (the existence of the Greys). Today, the Vatican has its own observatory and is happy to accept that other-worldly beings may exist, rather than burning its members for suggesting such things – such as was the fate of, for example, Giordano Bruno. Some might suggest that over time, the Church has modified its view in a more noticeable way than some modern scientists. It is interesting to note that when the various enquiries took place, the US Air Force anxiously tried to down play the phenomenon of UFOs. One of the senior US Air Force Officers on the panel was General Roger Ramey, who made it clear to Major Jesse Marcel what he should, or more pertinently should not, say with regard to the Roswell Incident that occurred a few years earlier.

The very active time of the UFO activity of the early fifties even reached into and affected the Head of the US Government. This can be evidenced in their decision to ban all aircraft from flying over the Whitehouse. However, the occupants of the alleged alien craft had no intention of being told where they could, or could not, fly and did so in large numbers over the Whitehouse. Naturally, the press made much of this and quite naturally asked angrily what the Air Force was doing about it? This was the time when the great 'debunking' exercise began. From this time onward, every alternative explanation was trotted out to account for the phenomena.

The Air Force had to get science on its side as soon as possible and people such as J Allen Hynek came along to encourage the scientific explanations. One of which he found difficult to live down after his complete conversation to convinced believer, was the 'swamp gas' theory. As for the radar returns, temperature inversions became the standard explanations. Radar operators were well aware of this phenomenon and made it clear that it did not explain their amazing radar returns in every case.

This progressive system of 'debunking' at all costs, reminds one of the statements made by President Lincoln, "You can fool some of the people all of the time and all of the people some of the time, but you can't fool all the people all of the time." One can quite understand the US Air Force's stance; they did not want it to appear that they could not defend US airspace. But the disturbing fact is that if the amazing flight capabilities of these mysterious craft was/is real, then they could not possibly defend it.

The Washington Whitehouse affair was a traumatic shock for the US and this was exacerbated when Hollywood saw the opportunity to cash in on the phenomena and, as a result, made many more people paranoid about the possible intention of the ETs. The films always seemed to concentrate on the oppression of the Earth and its peoples. For example, Invaders from space, Earth versus the Flying Saucers, War of the Worlds and so forth.

The aforementioned Dr Stephen Greer revealed some quite shocking, allegedly truthful facts, on a recent TV programme backed up by documentation and the various characters and their names who had made them. For example, Buzz Aldrin, one of the astronauts on Apollo 11, was said to have stated that an item that appeared to have been constructed, that he called a 'monolith', was photographed on the primary moon of Mars.

Dr Greer also covered the 'back engineering' process, said to be occurring in highly secretive bases such as Area 51, where scientists were allegedly poaching all the secrets of alien craft. Advanced aircraft designers, such as Ben Rich and Kelly Martin, would be aware of all this. One of the employees, and perhaps others (such as Boyd Bushman), worked for Lockheed Martin. So, the aforesaid designers would be more than happy to get their hands on such pieces of alleged UFOs. We only have to look at some of the aircraft designs that they came up with – from the U2 to stealth technology and the lower radar return – that were built into some of their designs.

These people would no doubt have extremely high security clearances, certainly above that of a President, but perhaps not as high as the faceless ones, the keeper of all the most vital secret information we are not privy to, whereas today, the secretive ones have closed ranks. The early members of the so-called Majestic Twelve sometimes stepped outside the policy, keeping everything to themselves and thought it was all too profound not to be gradually released to the people. Perhaps this was a little naïve, as most of us are aware how prone to panic, rioting, looting and destroying property many people are, but it does not follow that entire populations would behave in this manner. The offending group are always in a minority and are looked on with disgust, just as the earlier period of rampaging football fans did, when it seemed fashionable to do so, fortunately, the majority of well-behaved people see the futility of such negative behaviour, as it solves nothing, so a breakdown of society in general is not inevitable. However, serious consequences befell those that did advocate complete transparency on the ET hypothesis and the UFO phenomena and spoke up accordingly. They were quickly ostracised and out of the loop and vulnerable to being silenced in an extreme way.

The faceless ones, operating in the furtive clandestine way, must require funding and no doubt serious amounts of cash are diverted in their direction from the taxpayers' contributions. Of course, this also happens in Britain and many other countries who have to keep up with their defence estimates that are calculated by the top military defence chiefs, but they do not always get the amount they want.

However, it seems to be a different story in the US where the aforementioned Dr Stephen Greer stated that the US Government cannot account for twenty-five per cent of its money spent – of which no doubt a large portion will find its way to the secretive sect. We have to say that this Dr Greer must have many useful connections keeping him well informed about such matters. Many paradoxes have arisen in this whole analysis. One of which is that when George Bush Senior was head of the CIA, he actually was said to have refused to divulge all of the information his department had on the phenomena by presidential request. Yet later, George Bush himself became President. One would assume that during his presidency, he would not need to ask any questions because theoretically, he knew it all anyway. But did he know it all? As head of the CIA, no doubt he would have had access to much highly classified data, but, he would most likely have been 'outside the loop' of the secretive group who did not even trust presidents, or heads of the CIA or certainly the FBI, to be told everything.

We mentioned Jimmy Carter, who was quite adamant that he would lift all secrecy in regard to the UFO phenomena (as he had witnessed a sighting himself) when he became president. But it seems that he was quietly silenced when he did become president. To return to George Bush Senior, his son George W Bush also became President and would also be quite enlightened with regard to a lot of the secretive data that his father knew. When told, one wondered if his expression was as unrevealing as it was when he was informed about the terrorist attack on the Twin Towers (when a top aide came into the school classroom he was visiting). His eyes did not even widen.

One wonders what our alleged Greys think when observing all this horrific stupidity. Humanity forever destroying each other over issues that in times to come will seem so absurd. Furthermore, what do they think when they see one of their kind being sliced up on an operating table, if the frequently shown 'alien autopsy' is genuine footage? This is one of those examples that seems in one moment to be declared authentic, and then in the next is derided as fakery. Yet it seems to retain its place in the annals of the ufologists and conspiracy theories. The main factor against it is authenticity is that it is declared as being not too difficult for a film company's special effects department to duplicate quite easily.

If it is real footage, it would be the most profound thing that has ever happened on Earth. Many textbooks would surely be pouring off the presses in regard to alien biology and genetics, blood types, reproductive capabilities, vision, and general physiology – enough to fill the shelves of any medical centre. And surely medical researchers all over the world would be clamouring to gain as much information as possible, so their distancing from this topic speaks volumes.

However, if all the alleged Greys do eventually become a reality, then the aforesaid questions would all arise if science was allowed an opportunity to ask them. Certainly more so than the Church, whose questions would be in a different vein. If they knew of, or looked up to a higher presence themselves or subscribed to the view of a 'grand creator' and (obviously as well as science) would wish to know if, in their travels whether they ever encountered any other of 'gods creations', as they would, no doubt, accept that the Greys undoubtedly were.

Although we do not fully understand all the aspects of our own evolution, we certainly understand much about biology and physiology. We also have a deep understanding of the human genome, and we would most certainly wish to learn much about the physiology of the Greys if they do exist. Obviously, the main question by medical science and palaeoanthropology would be to solve the question once and for all, with regard to whether they had anything to do with our own origins, so that we may clear up all the unanswered questions pertaining to our own evolution. If they do exist, we would wish to know what ties them to Earth and whether it was their predecessors that were rising and descending in Bible times on 'Pillars of Fire.'

If humanity were to react in a sensible way in the face of their appearance and their revelations, and not react violently and see them as a threat, then a vast amount of knowledge could come our way. This could come about if the right type of preparation and good council was applied beforehand by those most qualified to handle it.

We would be most delighted to know about the flora and other life forms on their planet, and their own evolution. We may doubt that they eat or have ever eaten any of the other world life forms as we do on Earth. Our habit of eating other life forms likely seems abhorrent to them. It may be that they do not eat at all in the sense that we do. They could easily obtain their sustenance in other ways. In any case, when we consider the numerous descriptions of them emanating from the various abduction claims, their mouths, teeth and narrow jaws may have modified considerably over the probable lengthy evolution they have experienced; they may not even have teeth, which may have become evolutionarily redundant for them a long time ago.

With regard to the conditions on Earth, we could reflect on the distance between a virus and a sentient intelligent being, but that distance shrinks somewhat when we contemplate the fact that both operate in the same fashion by preying on other life in order to survive. A virus may kill its bodily host, but the virus will live on. And humans devour other creatures and living things in order to survive.

Even if one is a vegetarian, one still survives by eating living things that grow and exist in plant form, if an orange is left alone it will eventually drop off the tree, its seeds will penetrate the ground and it will reproduce another fruit bearing tree. But this process is interrupted when it is pulled from the tree, has its skin ripped off, and its bodily fluid squirts into the face of the attacker before it is torn apart and eaten.

Natural law set upon Earth is a hard law. Life becomes a merciless struggle – lifeforms survive at the expense of other life. The survival of the fittest. Lifeforms grow by devouring the weaker or less astute forms of life. Or, they even survive on the process of decay – summed up by the phrase, 'The finest roses are grown on dung.'

It would be most interesting to know about the natural processes that exist in their world and (if they do exist) science would be most curious about their evolution. For example, how old is it? Did they evolve in an unbroken line from a lesser lifeform in a process of natural selection? Did their intelligence slowly develop over millions of their years? Are there many mysteries regarding their past early history? Do they sense or know of a higher power? Did they come here in order to pass on the gifts of intelligence and creativity? If so, was it applied to their own forebears by beings unknown to them, that they see as advanced, highly intelligent creators? If so, could they pinpoint some period in their past evolution that showed a sudden burst of advancement and creativity in their evolution?

The eternal question on Earth is, are we the result of natural selection or some kind of unearthly intervention? Natural selection works fine for plants and flowers but not for the human. The results appear to favour an as yet undiscovered higher power that sees it as its duty to create more creators to explore the universe, find life, enhance and develop it. And that the process will continue throughout the cosmos in this manner for time immemorial. The process may have arisen on Earth without ever considering a divine creative God or an off-Earth intelligence, but the questions relative to the human evolutionary line would still be unanswered.

Similarly, if Kenneth Arnold, the private pilot who was responsible for the new term 'flying saucer', had simply got his sums wrong when calculating the speed that a group of objects that passed between the mountain peaks in 1947, the entire UFO syndrome may not have arisen. All the terms he used equated to a flock of geese, for example, 'silvery coloured', as geese and seagulls do when the sun shines on them, the undulating motion, the flapping of the wings and finally the crescent shape that he assigned to them and finally he never said that they were 'flying saucers', the press was responsible for that, he said that they flew like a saucer would if thrown across a pond.

In addition, if the object that may have been struck by lightning was a secret US project, all the activity that surrounded it would have taken place. The US Air Force (to use a colloquialism) 'shot themselves in the foot' by trotting out such an excuse as a weather balloon, simply because, as one person exclaimed, "Hell...even my dog can recognise a weather balloon." We may use as an analogy the people of Chad in Africa (for example), in the late early fifties had never seen (or at least never reported) any 'flying saucers', but with the advent of small transistor radios they caught up with the phenomena, then suddenly all the people of Chad were reporting them.

However, for all that an explanation is still required for the multitude of objects that do seem to be buzzing around the Earth would still have to be accounted for and we always have to enquire with regard to the root cause of it all, in particular the alleged abductions simply because of the numbers of people that claimed to have had such an encounter are immense.

The theory of our 'little grey men' whose predecessors brought about (many believe) the process of human evolution, has been well documented and written about and has much circumstantial evidence to support it. In addition, it is as good as any other explanation to account for the profound differences in the human that set us apart from any other creature. The odd fact is, there is not any other explanation at this time that can be offered to prove itself as more likely.

If it did happen that way, then links to the possibility that the Greys do exist among us, then adding all the factors together does add up to the necessity for a termination, final solution, end game, second coming revelations, or however we like to put it. Things cannot simply just go on as they are.

If, as some factors suggest, the secretive ones are working behind the scenes with the Greys. They would go to great lengths to keep their activities ultra secret and they do, but what happens when the Greys have got everything they want out of the bargain, which seems to be linked to the continuing human abductions, surely it will be the Greys who make the final decisions on any revelations or when they will finally appear to humanity. If their predecessors were involved in our very existence, they have a great responsibility to reveal it to us. The agenda of the secretive group is simple, obtain as much advanced technical information as possible, but the ultimate aim of the Greys may be far more important than that and it could even entail the very survival of their species when we refer to the many crash retrieval operations that occur in the US which are most certainly advanced experimental craft but not enough to stop them crashing. If they emanate from Area 51, the technical information they get from the secretive group allegedly working with the Greys may be third hand, and the second-hand tech information, that is, the data they gave to the secretive group, but they may be reluctant to give out all the secrets at once and hold back on vital data, otherwise there may not be so many alleged crash retrievals.

The shadowy group would have many scientists among their ranks who evaluate it and even they may assume it is all accurate and up to date, then pass it on to their counterparts in Area 51 and may not realise that vital data may be missing. All this would be going on behind the scenes and held from those in the most high office and certainly the masses who, of course, are ourselves. It may even be possible that the Greys do not want them to know, but just carry on with the pretence while progressing with their own agenda.

It has been stated that the unidentified group who knows all the answers and retains them, has a policy of L.D.D, or lie, deny and deceive. This is another name for the widespread 'black propaganda' that has occurred. In time, such a policy will undoubtedly come home to roost with them at some point in the future. If, as suggested, it all finally comes out, then these people once identified as those who kept us all in the dark may be ostracised and find it difficult to find a position where they would be fully trusted. This would apply mostly to the scientists. As for the others, they would no doubt slink back into the various security services. We have mentioned the so-called skunk works of Lockheed Martin and their super expensive advanced designs of flying craft. This activity does not come cheap and the enormous sums that disappear down the throat of the ever-open 'black hole' are diverted into certain advanced projects that are usually headed by very advanced thinking designers. It is always suggested that such places are being influenced by retrieved alien craft. If so, there would be far more to it than advanced aerodynamic design and low radar return built into such design. It is the power sources that are the main secrets which we may be very far from envisaging, let alone designing, may not be freely divulged by the Greys.

These companies and their designers are said to be responsible for the strange advanced craft observed darting in and out of Area 51 and no doubt learn from the mistakes that are responsible for the crashes and the subsequent retrievals that most people believe are UFOs. There is strong evidence that this so-called back engineering of UFO technology is taking place. And if it is, it clearly states the Greys are decidedly here – but not necessarily that the crash retrievals are alien craft. They could instead only be human attempts to duplicate their technology.

Perhaps the top designers frequently mentioned as Ben Rich and Kelly Johnston, are responsible for the remark that one 'loosed tongued' US Air Force officer made when he said, "We've got stuff out there fifty years ahead of anyone else." But although remarks such as this, and such as, "We'll soon have the technology to send ET back to where he came from," show that high technology exists, they also show that the old thinking, that ETs are a threat, is also still present. We would hope that there are not too many such people who still think like this, especially in high security posts. Nevertheless, it is doubtful that the alleged Greys would be too worried about it. It is just one more example of human failing and indicative of how rooted the fear of the unknown is ingrained in the human psyche. And such attitudes are not likely to exist in the upper hierarchies of the secret programmes, but rather, the officials with these beliefs would be working in their own restricted areas and would have learned about ETs only during 'canteen chatter.'

The Area 51 spotters who have got the closest of all the observers have noticed that one special airline transports the Area 51 workers in and out, and the pilots would simply land and take off again. The aircraft were identifiable with having a red strip running down the side, but little other identification. The passengers (or workers) are seen to disembark. The UFO watchers have tracked down a few of them and they say little (or know little) and state that they are driven to their place of work on coaches with blacked-out windows and stay in their work place until the work ceases, and then leave in the manner in which they came.

This is all rather like the 'cell system' that SOE and OSS in the US adopted in wartime; the system whereby even if an individual is viciously tortured, individuals can not reveal what other groups are involved in because they genuinely don't know. The IRA adopted the same system during their operations. We have speculated that the whole phenomenon may have begun in the one single incident that started the whole programme – in the incident that was the Roswell event. There were several witnesses that heard a tremendous 'explosion', or what we refer to as a 'thunderbolt', during an electrical storm the night before Mac Brazel found the widespread wreckage of shattered pieces. When collected for analysis, these pieces strangely exhibited almost indestructible qualities. Yet, they evidently could not resist the mighty force of nature when exposed to its full power. The storm must have caused a great disruption of the electronic power system in the craft.

However, the usual counter argument always arises, "Surely an advanced alien craft would know of and be prepared for such an event." A valid argument. After all, our own presumably far less advanced aircraft can withstand a lightning strike. To further analyse the remark, "We will soon have the technology to send ET back where he came from," could imply two things – firstly the knowledge that ET is here, and secondly the knowledge that the technology is reaching the stage at which that could happen. As mentioned, the worrying part of the statement is the 'sending back', which implies the use of force, which could have serious consequences.

However, we must hope that the person who made this remark was rebuked or severely censored. It primarily reflected bravado, but is nevertheless silly and dangerous. It is a bit worrying after all the advances of science, and a widening of our understanding in things cosmological, that we still have people who are firmly locked into this 1950s frame of mind - of 'earth versus the flying saucers' kind of thinking.

However, it may have some effect on the plans and thinking of the alleged Greys when it comes to what could be called the final showdown. It still remains risky to write off the so-called Roswell incident when real people documented and named were involved – such as the local mortician, Glenn Dennis, who was asked to produce a number of small coffins. Such items would obviously not be asked for to accommodate balloon wreckage, or wooden crash test dummies or monkeys with their hair burned off. It was this kind of continual changing of the explanation regarding the Roswell incident that plays into the hands of the conspiracy theorists.

If we refer again to the select few or secret operatives that are in possession of the real data, with security classifications far above the FBI, the CIA and the Defence Agencies, even the President, then they must be very smart and intelligent people. So we must ask, why does this high intelligence prevent them from concluding some kind of preparation ought to be gradually applied to humanity in order to 'soften the blow', as it were, when such a culmination of it all must finally occur?

All of this 'need to know' nonsense will only make their job so much more difficult, if or when the 'game changing' event does take place and as it will very much affect all of humanity, we certainly do need to know. If they are not prepared to take on this task, then let the Church handle it. We will discuss this further in the chapter, 'The Church and the Greys.'

If the masses were slowly introduced to all of the interesting questions that could be answered if we 'listened' rather than reacted in panic and violence, then the human mindset could be suitably tuned to the positive side in preparation. Such a process could be initiated gradually and quietly in a series of interesting TV programmes. These would not immediately admit the presence of the Greys on our planet, but would introduce a 'what if' mode of thinking. It would introduce humans to all the ways in which we could be helped by this phenomenon and would help to avoid the potential negative effects of such revelations that would come out of the worst side of humanity – panic, looting and destruction. The author, Rene Noorbergen, in his book Secrets of the Lost Races, remarked on the dichotomy between our negative and destructive qualities on the one hand, and being supremely equipped in other ways. He asks the following questions: "Did they really visit us in ancient times?" "Is our current technology a mere shadow of what 'they' once taught us in ancient times?" And, "Is it possible that the highly technical ancient artifacts that attest to a super technology (Ooparts) of another world actually belong to our own ancient historical development?"

Noorbergen implies that humanity may have actually regressed over the millennia rather than evolved. Even as advanced as we obviously are, we may have lost more than we have gained. Also (history repeating itself), are we now approaching a level of advancement and sophistication that ultimately led to a historical downfall in our remote past?

These are all valid questions and could be answered along with many others by our alleged Greys. It could be that much that transpired during the dawn of human history is now lost beneath the rubble of our distant past. We all are aware of the purposeful destruction of knowledge that existed right up to the period of the Red Revolution and the masses all dressed the same and acting like automatons in the era of Mao Tse Tung and burning books in their thousands.

It is quite amazing to think that this kind of thing could have been going on such a short time ago in comparison to historical time periods. We have made the assumption that the Greys have, in an arrangement with the secretive ones, revealed much high technological and advanced data in return for an uninterrupted process of abductions of humans and (for whatever reasons) the frequent removal of bovine blood and cattle's reproductive organs, which obviously indicates something of importance to them. We have said that they may have been cunning enough to only release what they want to release. After all, they would not wish to play into the hands of people who brag about soon being able to 'send them back to where they came from.'

That would have been a source of embarrassment to the secretive ones, who would, no doubt have to placate their 'little grey partners' that the person in question would be suitably dealt with. It seems that there maybe two levels of activity occurring, one with a far higher security grading than the other. The highest level being the joint operation between the faceless few and the Greys and what they allow to filter down to the operatives in Area 51.

Rene Noorbergen's remark in the aforesaid book is very apt: "We have made our current century both an age of development and an age of high confusion." It doesn't follow that the alleged Greys have revealed all that they know to the secretive few. In fact, it is most unlikely and if a final 'end game' does occur, together with many profound revelations, then what they might reveal may stun their human partners just as much as anyone else.

Surely, the unresolved question of our own human origins (assuming they may know it in the first place) would be one of, if not the most important question we would like answered. For many years, we have been living with various theories – from Einstein's relativity, to time warps, to wormholes in space, and many other scientific concepts. These theories do rest on valid principles and are deemed mathematically possible, yet our supposed human development from protoplasm, to ape, then to man, is still the subject of widespread controversy and discussion. With this in mind, one would think that instead of pretending that the Darwinian concept for the appearance of humans is all resolved, that widespread discussion and debate should prevail. There should be open-mindedness to an alternative instead of energetically attempting to 'humanise' apes in intensive training programmes and constantly referring to them as our 'cousins'. Anthropologists themselves have said that, "it is doubtful that men were ever apes in the true sense, the differences are too great and numerous." It is surely a very bad policy to ignore issues that puzzle us rather than attempting to resolve them. The business of the 'Ooparts' is a prime example. There is no doubt that a very ancient yet highly technically advanced society did once exist on Earth, so it is natural to ask was it a human culture or otherwise? Another question to put the Greys if ever the opportunity arises.

It has been suggested that these objects bear testament to the existence of a past super civilisation of human origin at some distant point in the history of humankind. It is easy to assign these artifacts as being extra-terrestrial in origin, but none of them are composed of material unknown on Earth. Yet, any planet in the echospheral zone of a sun-like star that may be inhabited by intelligent creative entities, would be living on a planet that would almost certainly be made up of the same material that is universal throughout the cosmos and no doubt quite similar to earthly material, which is also contained within our very bodies, and no doubt theirs.

Moreover, who is to say that the hypothetical ETs did not manufacture them on Earth rather than bringing them along with them, they would be fairly sure that Earth would contain all the materials they needed such as metals, ceramics, anything they required. With this hypothesis, of course, we are always in danger of a denigration of the capabilities of the ancients. The Bible mentions that amazing longevity of the patriarchs, so, in their long lives, spanning centuries, they could well have developed a very highly sophisticated technology.

We must also consider the fact that a cosmic disaster may have befallen the Earth in the past, putting humanity back into the Stone Age. The ancient Egyptian priests did, in fact, preach that this kind of event did happen and was not only a singular occurrence and that the result was that humankind had to begin all over again starting as children learning. These kinds of remarks clearly indicate the ancientness of the Egyptian historical knowledge, which includes their own advancement and its destruction. The Genesis story of the flood is one example that ancient historians did record and not only in the Biblical Middle East, but all over the world. This calamitous event would have to be so destructive and so complete that it would stretch our imagination to even contemplate it.

If the ancient Egyptians were so sure of all these disasters of pre-history, then obviously there must have been survivors in order for them to record it in their long historical records. There are always survivors in any disaster. All of this, of course, would be very well known to our hypothetical Greys. Their memory banks would be replete with data and no doubt not only pertaining to earthly matters, especially if we accept the possibility that their creative endeavours and skills of their forebears produced the advanced human species in the first place. Their memory banks would dwarf any other historical records, such as the Egyptian dynasties.

We would have to consider that the Greys may have historical data going back for at least fifty thousand years or shortly before the special qualities in the advanced human creation manifested themselves in the onset of human cultural evolution. This makes it clear that rather than fearing the possibility of an ET presence with negative destructive and retaliatory type of thinking, we should dwell on the positive and more enlightening information. We could be made aware of and how it would advance our species in a very short time and make us ready for the big adventure taking us out of our solar system all together. After all, that would surely have been the ultimate aim of the ancient human experiment in the first place. Yet we still have the humans who are in jobs that perhaps they should not be in, stating naïve remarks about belligerent retaliatory action again ETs. This is Stone Age thinking from the time when defence from other humans was always uppermost in the mind.

If there is any future at all for humankind, we must not allow people to retain important positions, while still making remarks that only reflect the savage nature of our past. This could reflect the very part of the human psyche that the hypothetical 'creators' wished to eliminate and no doubt, so long after their own predecessors completed the 'human experiment', the present day Greys who may be among us could do so, quite easily.

Ancient legends are so steeped in accounts referring to 'gods' who came from the sky, are so abundant that they would fill volumes, somewhere hidden among this mass of data or massive jigsaw puzzle, if we could find all the right pieces and put them together, the whole picture of the human story might be revealed to us.

One piece of the jigsaw is the story of Genesis, allegedly written by Moses. The strange factor is, and which we commented on in other work, Moses lived for a long time in Egypt in the Pharaonic household for a good part of his life, that is from the legendary rescue of his 'babe in the basket' infancy to maturity yet his account seems to bear no resemblance to what we might expect with regard to Egyptian historical events, they were all concerned with the Hebrew. Moses was educated in Egypt, yet the Divine Creator he spoke of was nothing to do with an Egyptian deity. After his banishment and subsequent return to Egypt to free the Hebrews he had little time to spare to sit writing the extensive data that makes up the Genesis story and he even died before reaching his promised land,

and before he was well occupied with battling his way through the desert wilderness, Mount Sinai, the Commandments and the Ark of the Covenant, the destruction of Jericho and so forth are all accepted as being written by Moses as he himself was in the thick of it, but the creation story does not reflect his long education period. The Egyptian tutors must have taught him a great deal about the lengthy Egyptian history and records and all of their 'gods', but as said, none of that is reflected in his Genesis account dealing with creation.

One may wonder how much, if any, of this kind of data would have been revealed to the mysterious ones who secretly kept all the profound data of the phenomena to themselves. It is entirely possible that the alleged Greys themselves may have instructed them to do so and that the Greys themselves will decide when the time is right for their eventual appearance, and what should be told to the masses.

As said, we cannot have one without the other. If these beings do exist, there must be a final chapter. This may well be decided by their hierarchy in their own world. Such beings would have had plenty of time to have regretted not issuing the order long ago instead of the situation today where humans could cause so much unnecessary trouble for them, particularly when it is exacerbated by giving humans even more advanced non-earthly technology. As said, extremely advanced or not, they will be, in some sense, vulnerable.

However, there would be only so much that they would tell to scientific members of the secretive group that are among the 'silent' ones (or would wish to tell) and the completion of their entire programme may be drawing to a close. Two factors would seem to reinforce this conclusion, firstly, the careless, 'off the cuff' remarks, about humans soon having the technology to equal that of the Greys and secondly the revelation to a female abduction victim who claimed she was informed by the Greys that their earthly operations were 'drawing to a close'.

We could speculate on many ways in which they could go about it, but only 'they' will know. such beings could, as early as tomorrow, instruct the faceless ones to begin slowing filtering all the documents the previously held and also the readable copies that they blacked out when pretending to comply with the Freedom of Information Act. Everything would have to be done in a gradual fashion when we consider the excitable and easily disturbed groups among humanity.

Around two thousand years ago all of this gradual preparation would not have been necessary at all, the masses were eager and ready for it and had after all been told that it was imminent, but, for some reason the final decision was postponed by 'planet heaven', causing great embarrassment to the patriarchs, who became ostracised as 'false prophets'.

Two thousand years ago, the Emissary on Earth whom we know as Jesus, made it clear that the time was nigh when he stated in Mathew XXIV 34 and Mathew X23 (when referring to the second coming and the revelations), "Verily I say unto you, this generation shall not pass 'till all these things be fulfilled, ye shall not have gone over the cities of Israel 'till the son of man become." However, Jesus made it clear that nobody knew the exact date when all of this would come to pass, "No, not the angels in heaven, but my father only" (the home planet ruler?).

In another work we suggested that part of the hypothetical deal struck between the Greys and the faceless ones or select few, may have included a deal where the greys could carry out all the human abductions they needed for their programme as long as the humans were returned unhurt, and they were, but not necessarily 'mentally'. The purpose may have been to invigorate their own species. Perhaps with the use of human haemoglobin. Strangely, they must also possess a large amount of bovine blood extracted from the numerous carcases of cows found drained of their blood. Also, of the abductions have been going on since the sixties (and they have), then by now they must possess many barrels of the stuff. In a recent TV programme, it was stated that cattle have long strands of DNA equal to human DNA.

If, as the theory suggests, the forebears of the alleged Greys utilised part of their own bodily makeup, to develop humanity but now their own bodies are degenerating, they may feel we owe them something in return for the 'enhancing' process in order to provide humans with high intelligence and creativity that so many of us are able to use today. In short, it is 'payback time'. This is of no detriment to humanity and we ought to be happy to oblige their body form on their own world may be showing positive regeneration due to this hypothetical operation.

If the faceless group do start, a programme involving the gradual release of all the information that they have held for so long no one could say that they have not done a top class security job in the protection of all the secret information, no matter how much we resented their methods. However, as we have said, it may have been part of the (possible) 'deal', agreed between the secretive ones and the Greys who may have made it clear that they did not want to see any disruption of their own programme by any (in modern parlance) 'whistle blowers' before their operations are completed. Incidents like the abduction victim being told by the Greys that their operations were now drawing to a close did not take place only recently; this was mentioned in a book specifically dealing with alleged abductions some time ago. This raises a couple of questions. Is the time of the revelations now decades overdue? Imminent? Or are we to consider that perhaps another postponement has been ordered from the ETs' own world? In this regard, we have two interesting factors to consider, firstly the indications are that a huge unidentified craft has entered our solar system (which we will expand upon shortly). Secondly, if the Greys and their predecessors had actually been involved in causing the mental advancements and capabilities of the human race for so long, then it is entirely possible that many others of their species reside under the Earth, within the Moon, and/or under the surface of Mars (which would explain all those methane emissions). Many, or all, of these beings may never have experienced life on their 'mother' planet.

When humans eventually colonise Mars, people will be born there that may never know what it's like to reside on Earth. Perhaps the huge craft will enable them to go 'home' sometimes. What is the evidence for this possible 'mother ship' that has entered into a strange earthly orbit? It has been said to resemble the shape of a cigar and has been photographed in orbit about the Earth. It was stated that it is not an asteroid or even from our solar system, but that it originates from elsewhere in the galaxy. It was stated that NASA did not release the photographs taken. Its polar orbit would allow it to observe all the Earth as it rotated. Its shape precludes any postulation of being an asteroid. The hypothetical appearance of humanoid entities, whichever way we look at it, would be an extremely traumatic event for humanity to endure. And, if our Greys have been with us on Earth for as long as the evidence suggests, then they would know better than anyone else how humanity would be likely to react. This indicates that the time is now, and that the secretive ones should come in from the cold and begin, either themselves or hand it to the Church, an intensive preparation and counselling for humans on the positive factors to be gained.

Once the population becomes aware of the very long time period that the Greys have already been involved in earthly matters, then it should become clear to the masses that subjugation is not their aim. To soften the blow, the great advancements that await us in technology, in medical science (and in cures for cancer, dementia etc), should be emphasised.

Nevertheless, the possibility does exist that we humans may act in the predictable way, and our savage tendencies might cause some of us to explode into looting and pillaging. If this happens, it will not be the secretive group who has to bear the brunt of these effects; it would be the law enforcement agencies, the National Guard, and the military, rather than those who are responsible for it due to their secrecy.

We have said in the chapter regarding 'The Church and the Greys', that if the pre-revelations period of preparation was handled correctly, it may even result in humanity looking forward to the event instead of reacting in a violent way. There is, of course, the possibility that the home planet of the Greys may make a decision where they feel that there would be no need to risk any of the above scenarios and just withdraw their operatives completely. After all, they may have got what they needed from humanity and perhaps got more out of it than the secretive group who are so frequently having to recover their faulty back engineered craft. The Greys would know that humans, as it stands, are not one hundred per cent ready to join the cosmic club.

We have said that the Greys would also be aware that, due to their predecessors' efforts, humans are a lot closer to the ability to cure the negative aspects still prevail in the human brain than they are to stepping off into the cosmos. Therefore, the experts using the fast-advancing knowledge in biological processes, the stem cell research, and the human genome can complete the job themselves (rather than hoping that the Greys would do the job in a clandestine way). After all, one hospital patient who had a 'near death experience,' was told by the creatures during his experience that humans were bestowed with the power to heal themselves long ago.

In this scenario, it would be down to the select group who had been working secretly with the Greys to reveal all to the public after they had departed. One would imagine that it would be far less traumatic for most humans to hear from other humans, that ETs were responsible for our origins, rather than hearing this directly from ETs.

Nevertheless, it must have been just as traumatic for many people when humans were told quite pedantically by science that any idea of 'divine creation' was unscientific and just mysticism. "Your ancestors were apes and not due to an unknown creator waving a majestic hand ... live with it." But there would still be a noticeable backlash and angry feeling toward the silent ones who had prevented the population from having the choice to reject or accept the amazing revelations of 'the greys,' or prevented them from seeing them for themselves (apart from of course the abduction victims). The Greys would know that humanity, as it stands, is not one hundred per cent ready to join the cosmic club.

And what would happen to the secret groups who had worked with the Greys? When these faceless ones dispersed into the background, the security section of the group would fare better with their proven security abilities, they would be happily absorbed back into the various groups such as the CIA, the FBI, the National Defence Agency, and many other posts such as naval intelligence, the army intelligence corps and various posts in the Pentagon.

It would be the scientists who would fare the worst, even if they did obtain posts in foreign technology analysis, or places such as Area 51. Mainstream science would (as they are only human) resent them the most. Such scientific members of these silent ones may have belonged to the same golf club as others they knew. They may have had a few drinks with them, yet did not trust them to have the 'need to know' of these things. In any case, the mainstream scientists would not know if such a group may still exist. But in this hypothetical situation, the power would be back where it belongs – in the hands of an elected government and a president or prime minister who had been elected by the people.

To conclude this chapter, the same quotations that I copied in my book, High Strangeness would be very apt here – especially if there is no culmination at hand and the silent ones continue in their same old way. Thomas Aquinas stated, "It is entirely legitimate to hide from the masses the holy and secret truth about the spirits of a higher order than man."

CHAPTER II

THE CHURCH AND THE GREYS

When the astronomers who have their facility in the Vatican, are looking through their telescopes and are not afraid to admit that extra-terrestrial life is possible, or that 'gods children' may be among us on Earth, they must feel quite guilty when reflecting that their predecessors a couple of centuries ago happily burned people alive for these beliefs. For example, people who were not afraid to stand for what they believed, such as Giordano Bruno and other victims.

It is plain to see that the Church has moved faster than other areas – faster than people generally and the scientific mainstream – in modifying their views with regard to the phenomena of extra-terrestrials and their possible existence on Earth. Young modern-thinking Bible students, when reflecting on the actions of beings described as 'angels', may in some case, 'cross the floor' (to use a political phrase) and change their allegiance with regard to their interpretation of the 'angels' entirely due to their decidedly non-Biblical activity with regard to the humans and perhaps even accept the ET hypothesis. In my book, Pillars of Fire, I set out to analyse the actions and interactions between 'angels', the patriarchs in the Bible, and special types of human. The writers of the ancient scriptures did not minimise or play down the decidedly non-earthly actions of the angels because everything they did was simply classified as 'divine'. Unlike today, where certain events are definitively played down, with every alternative explanation given except the one that they think might disturb us with regard to the obviously unearthly technology of the various UFO phenomena.

In Pillars of Fire, I made it quite clear that the Biblical angels during the time of patriarchs (patriarchs such as Abraham, Moses and many others throughout both the Old and New Testaments) bore no resemblance to the rosy-cheeked beings that we think of as angels – with their wings, innocent expressions, golden hair and long white apparel. This image was portrayed in the religious icons, paintings, and drawings by the religious artists of the Middle Ages and eventually adopted by Christmas card designers everywhere.

One can deeply research the writings of the Bible, both the Old and the New Testaments, and one will not encounter a single reference to the angels flapping about with the use of wings in order to interact with the Biblical patriarchs. The method that the angels used to descend and arise after their communications with the patriarchs was, as the title of my book Pillars of Fire suggests, with some kind of device strapped to the person. This is quite amazing in itself when we ourselves have only fairly recently developed this technology for use (originally by the military).

For those who wish to obtain a copy of my book, Pillars of Fire, I will not repeat the very modern methods the angels used when descending to fulfil their special operations except to say that one of their specialities was to inseminate even barren women to produce special being whose tasks on Earth had already been planned-for.

We have said that the Church has already moved forward much faster than the masses, and even science itself, with regard to its attitude and stance of the existence of the beings we have chosen to call the Greys. Many people, including scientists, still think the whole UFO and abduction phenomenon is nonsense. The Church does not necessarily believe that the Greys are here on Earth, but to accept that the phenomenon is real, must surely demand acceptance of this idea. So, we are faced with the possibility that highly intelligent beings, who are obviously quite advanced, are on the Earth, but not a product of it.

Nevertheless, the Church still seems reluctant to discuss or highlight the signs of an advanced technology that was displaying itself on Earth a couple of thousand years ago in the days of the patriarchs. In particular, the amazing events before, during, and after the exodus saga that takes up a large part of the Old Testament – the story that is so 'extra-terrestrial' in nature. The Church simply leaves it to others to interpret these events as they wish and form their own conclusions, but all this Biblical data is the 'bread and butter' of the Theologists and therefore intensely studied in the ecclesiastical colleges. It must be discussed, picked over, and argued about?

To point to just one example. Moses was actually informed and warned of the dangers that might befall the Hebrews if they did not keep back when their craft was landing on Mount Sinai. Beings 'not of this Earth' made it clear to Moses that they would arrive and descend in a thick cloud on the mountain and any inquisitive Hebrews who broke through the cordon that Moses was told to set up would be 'shot through.'

Clouds were often used to hide craft in, and were most likely artificially produced by the craft itself. Even Jesus himself on his last days on Earth rose up into one. The so-called tabernacle that Moses was given precise instructions to construct was immense enough to hide their craft when it descended (once again) in a cloud. It was constructed well away from the Hebrews' gaze. All that they saw was an eerie phosphorescent glow when the beings were inside communicating with Moses. It also contained the Ark of the Covenant built by Moses that was also an 'oracle', or communication device, to keep in contact with the extra-terrestrials. All of this data must be the subject of lengthy discussion on the theological centres. It cannot simply be ignored.

The ETs, or Greys, went to a lot of trouble with regard to the tabernacle – even with regard to the depictions on its outer surface. It was to be decorated with images of the beings that interacted with Moses and, no doubt, the other patriarchs. That is, the beings we are used to being told were 'angels', which simply means messenger. The beings depicted on the tabernacle's outer covers were called 'cherubim' or 'cherubs'.

When Ezekiel had his famous encounter with beings 'not of this Earth', he used the same words to describe them. With regard to this tabernacle, the French author, Paul Thomas, when writing of it, stated that it was three hundred cubits in length. That is a huge construction which equates in imperials measurement to four hundred and fifty feet. This is the same length as the alleged Ark of Noah and certainly large enough to accommodate any craft that descended from Mount Sinai.

One can read an account of the main craft and its descent onto Mount Sinai in impressive detail in exodus XIX 16-18. It confirms the threat to any 'nosy parkers' or adventurous Hebrews that may be thinking of sneaking up the mountain to have a quick peek at the craft; they would be killed, pure and simple. Earlier, data on this event is contained in exodus XIX 12-13. Few people today think that the Bible is just a collection of old legends. The Church seems content to let the events and discoveries by excavations speak for themselves, and they do. The Bible cannot be dismissed as unreliable with regard to its passages. Entire cities that were mentioned in the Holy Writ, whose only existence had formerly been only simple conjecture, have been discovered over the years.

Just one example of this was the discovery of the city of Ur in Mesopotamia, said to be the birthplace of Abraham. We might also mention the discovery of the city of Megiddo, which is the root of the word Armageddon, is supposedly located at the spot where the final 'second coming' or conflagration will occur. In this ancient city of Megiddo, the remains of successive civilisations have been found one on top of another. The wonders and richness of the Biblical King Solomon may not have been exaggerated; in the excavated level alleged to have been contemporaneous with the King, magnificent stables were found that were built with plans similar to modern stables and they would have accommodated around four hundred and fifty horses. Obviously, these stables were connected to, or were the property of, a person of great power and wealth.

If we return to the huge craft whose landing was described in such detail in Exodus, we are tempted to see it as more like fitting into a science fiction story than a Biblical event. But such attention to detail often occurs in these stories – such as in the precise dates and times mentioned in Ezekiel's experience. Moses was careful to mention, with regard to the strange craft that landed on Mount Sinai, that it occurred on the first day of the first month of the second year. One must assume if it was Moses that wrote all of this data, that he would have been just as meticulous in his other writings. Since Moses was the patriarch who led the whole exodus event, naturally he would have been the one most qualified to write it, yet some Biblical scholars state that it is clear that other hands were at work when compiling the scripts.

One supposes that such scholars on the ancient scriptures can detect when a certain style of writing suddenly changes. Other experts during World War 2 could, it is said, detect the style of Morse Code messages from their agents and could tell if someone else had taken over the key. To return to Moses' account, the angels' objective was referred to as 'Palestina', not 'Canaan', as was the ancient name for Israel. This indicates that they intended to possess an Arabian country. However, all throughout the story of their great trek, the extra-terrestrial connotations are always there. And there is always the same attention to detail with regard to times and dates when referring to the aforementioned tabernacle that Moses had received explicit instructions to build.

"And it came to pass on the twentieth day of the second month, in the second year, that the cloud was taken up from off the tabernacle of the testimony." At that point, the wonder weapon of the Hebrews, that is the Ark of the Covenant, was inside the tabernacle. It must have been brought down by the 'angels' hidden in the craft that was shrouded in mist. Although Moses had constructed it under the tuition of the 'angels' in his forty-day course in the craft when it was perched on the mountain, all he brought down were the Tablets of the Ten Commandments.

In my book Pillars of Fire, I refer to the possibility that the first set of Tablets that Moses threw down in disgust (and were broken), could still be there under layers of windblown sand, and that a specific quest by a latter day 'Indiana Jones' could possibly find them. Certainly, an easier quest than attempting to find the Ark of the Covenant. Moses was provided with a new set later in the story. A great punishment was metered out to the Hebrews that the returning Moses witnessed when he descended and observed their misdemeanours when they turned away from 'Yahweh', their own true god. The punishment cost the lives of three thousand Hebrews. It does not seem likely that any alleged extra-terrestrial entities like the Greys would have condoned this severe act. One would have thought that other punishments would suffice; they had done nothing that warranted a death sentence.

Obviously, the Greys would surely have observed the undesirable qualities of humans, yet they did not stop these actions. Very strange. Some kind of court of enquiry must have occurred to sort out the guilty parties. The brother of Moses, Aaron, had surely failed himself when being left in charge of the Hebrews in the absence of Moses up in the mountain for forty days. It is strange in any case that the Hebrews could have turned away so easily from the amazing powers of 'Yahweh' that they had witnessed. Shortly before this lapse, the Hebrews were quaking in their boots when witnessing the arrival of the unearthly craft onto the mountain that they accepted as 'the glory of Yahweh'.

On top of this, they had also witnessed the amazing spectacle of the parting of the Red (Reed) Sea, so that they could get across safely out of harm's way. That is, away from the wrath of the Pharaoh's army. So it makes little sense that they could turn away from such power so easily and worship false gods. Also, they had witnessed first-hand this great power descending dramatically down into the tabernacle (a type of hanger) so that the 'angels' or unearthly visitors could bring down the Ark of the Covenant or communication device to Moses in order to discuss strategy. Since this tabernacle was so large and intricately designed, it must have been a rather tedious process to keep having to erect, then dismantle, before the Hebrews moved on. Exodus makes it clear that when the 'angels' rose up and returned to the 'mother ship' they moved forward, following a column of light.

Exodus makes it clear when describing this dismantling process that it was "Taken down by skilled workmen belonging to the families of Gershom and Merari in pieces and placed in the centre of the caravan." The pillar of cloud obviously made some kind of communication to Moses, probably via the 'oracle' or receiver in the Ark, when the angels decided to stop. Then the Hebrews had to make camp and put everything back together again, but no doubt as the Hebrews were so substantial in numbers (already when they left Egypt and by now even more so) they would soon complete the work quite efficiently by working together.

It was necessary to make these frequent stops in order for the plan and operations the 'angels' had in mind to be talked over and discussed with Moses, Aaron and Joshua as the leaders of 'operation exodus.' All the forthcoming battles and conflicts that had to be confronted or avoided, and that seem so extra-terrestrial in nature, must have been discussed by the Church scholars. This may happen in the close confines of an ecclesiastical college, but not, it would seem, from the average pulpit. They would not be able to avoid the extra-terrestrial connotations that occur throughout these events and since the Church readily accepts the existence of extra-terrestrials, it would seem to be an easy conversion from 'theologist' to 'ufologist'. But to return to the Biblical events. The Greys at that time must have had other operations in progress, no doubt far from Earth. At various times, the Bible mentions 'quiet times' when there was a noticeable absence of the Greys. This would only be one of many questions that would be cleared up if or when there is ever a culmination of it all, but much more important questions would take precedent.

This is of course, if humanity chose to listen rather than to violently react, but as we have said, this would depend on the effectiveness of the preconditioning and preparation process that was introduced beforehand when we mentioned the 'quiet times' that is the noticeable absence of the Greys and their activities. In the Old Testament there is a phrase used in the Book of Kings, that describes this absence of the 'beings in the clouds', it states 'there was no open vision'. The children of Israel at these times had to rely on tales and stories related to them, which many of them would struggle to believe that their fathers and grandfathers preached to them regarding their past experiences.

One could imagine the children listening with wide-eyed wonderment and an elder stating, "Then Moses the leader of our ancestors raised his magic rod, and the waters piled high on both sides, then after we had crossed safely, he turned, rose his staff again and our enemies were drowned to a man." The young audience would in some cases look at each other in disbelief, yet those same stories would no doubt still be preached today in the many synagogues a couple of thousand years later with the young listeners probably believing every word.

It is entirely possible, as we said in 'Pillars of Fire' that the chosen and notable figures in the Old Testament and the other scriptures that we know as the patriarchs could have been purposely created beings (hybrids if you like) with subservient genes, in order to obey without question the instructions given to them by the beings we now refer to as the Greys. Their particular role in life was previously mapped out for them. They would have served their masters fully when they were elsewhere in the cosmos, perhaps nurturing intelligence in other suitably evolving beings apart from the patriarchs already functioning. It seemed as though the Greys thought it necessary to have further representation on Earth and they singled out the infant Samuel to receive a 'signal' that may have been some kind of 'brain waive' or previously inserted mental input to be activated on command at a later date to 'activate' him so to speak.

Samuel received a message that came from a specific area of the Ark or 'oracle', as it also functioned as the receiver unit. From the area just above the lid, that is between the wings of the outstretched cherubim fixed to the lid, came the voice of 'Yahweh'. When it was installed in the Temple of Solomon, he was able to communicate by the use of the device above the Ark.

From around 1040 BC, it was some eighty years had to pass before the 'cloud' reappeared in all its splendour, and once more took up residence on Earth, that is, in the safety of the Temple of Solomon, who had built the Temple primarily for this purpose. It seems that the strong mental input we mentioned to Samuel (Solomon's father) set this train of events in motion. In those times, everything that happened seemed to occur in a prearranged pattern, set up by the 'angels' long ago. Certainly this was the case in (or before) the time of Abraham, who had been under the control of the 'angels' since his youth and followed their orders without question. If we consider that the Greys are the descendants of those operatives of Biblical times, then if more people took the trouble to analyse and interpret these obviously unearthly events in another way than intended by the scribes, then it should become clear that beings 'not of this Earth' have been very active in the affairs of humans all the way back to our origins. If this were examined, then more and more people would begin to see a different message than what they currently believe the Bible is all about. This is not to detract from, or be disrespectful of, people's views that it is all the holy word of God. They are quite entitled to this belief. We are speaking in terms of adding to the preparation or mental assessment of the events that were happening in Biblical times and prepare for a culmination to it all in order to make it clear, possibly by the Greys themselves, that it was their predecessors who were active in those times and to correct all the misunderstandings.

Naturally, the Churchmen would not be entirely happy with this, having to re-assess all that they have studied, believed in and followed, not to mention taught to the masses only to find it was all wrong. But if they do accept the existence of the Greys, then they would have to consider all of this. If people in general did accept all these Biblical events as extra-terrestrial in nature, then they must consider that the perpetrators could not simply go away; their descendants have inherited a great responsibility for the human race and must, in the form of their present-day beings, still reside in the vicinity of the Earth. This would also make it clear that their objective was not to dominate and take the Earth for themselves, but rather the opposite, to help and assist humankind. And if the Church preached this kind of message, it would greatly assist in any kind of 'end game' or conclusion to the ETs' programme here on Earth. Strangely, when we consider how long ago it occurred, some fairly recent observations that we will shortly relate, are noticeably similar to the Biblical descriptions of the column of light, dust or cloud or whatever it was comprised of, that the Hebrews observed during the exodus saga. The cloud descending into the tabernacle and later leading the Hebrews with a vertical column of luminous gas or mist is not a past event with regard to that description. As the Hebrews trekked toward their ultimate goal or Promised Land, they followed this pillar of cloud that had some interior source of energy as it glowed like a light beacon or starlight shining down to the ground at night to show them the way.

The UFO sightings previously mentioned have also been described as vertical columns made of material that was described as cloudy or opaque. Often mentioned with these sightings are 'discs' reported to either circle around the cloud or enter and leave it. Sometimes the vertical column was said to be in motion, in the sense of whirling or spiralling as though some inner force was agitating it.

Some of these cases are well documented. For example, on July 23rd 1952, a vertical 'cylinder' that was described as 'a silvery' was seen to swallow two discs. This was observed above Culver City in California. Similarly, another object that was also described as cylindrical also accompanied by flying discs was observed above Denmark in September of the same year. Germany, Norway and Sweden also received reports of a similar nature. If this object was some kind of mother craft, suggested by the discs moving in and out of it, why so close to the ground? It is usual for objects described as mother craft to be in high orbit.

The Church and the Greys

It seems that the Greys have various types of craft at their disposal. A very strange case of this nature occurred again on October 16th 1952. The habitants of Oloron in the Basses Pyrenees reported (which included the Mayor and the Masters of the local school). A long cylinder in a cloudless sky giving off a trail of white 'smoke' and a series of discs moved around it. The 'procession' passed slowly by, then disappeared. Then another cylinder in a vertical position shone brightly for half an hour with discs, 'coming in and out of it all the time.' It was moving against the direction of the wind above heads of the Vendêans on September 14th 1954. This data was recorded by Aimê Michel who had provided all the details of the UFO sightings in all those straight lines across the continent of France.

The comparison to the Biblical description of the column that moved before the Hebrews as they trekked across the desert after Exodus is quite apparent. The French author Paul Tomas, when commenting on strange Biblical occurrences, stated in his book, Flying Saucers Through the Ages, "It was not a simple flying saucer that led the Hebrews during their exodus, it was something quite exceptional, a cylindrical mother ship described as a pillar of cloud. It was accepted by the Hebrews as 'the glory of Yahweh'." Clearly, many people will point out that our Greys if existing in Earth-space today, would not be likely to be utilising technology in fairly recent times that they employed when interacting with humans in Biblical times. But we would point out, as we have done in other work, that we are concerning ourselves with earthly time. The Greys, or at least their predecessors, would most likely have been, and perhaps still are, concerned with other operations far from Earth and may be capable of enormous speed or alternative ways of travel. It is mathematically accepted that time itself could be altered when moving away from Earth at a tremendous velocity and occupants of such craft would not age, whereas Earth would. It has been described as 'time dilation' and was depicted in the film Close Encounters of the Third Kind, where the occupants of Flight 19 were returned at the same age as they were in 1945.

The Church will always be in a possession of its trump card in the shape of an almighty creator we all know as a divine God. If traumatic revelations did occur, we have to ask how would the Church react to our 'grey aliens' – and to the idea that aliens might have been the grand creators of humanity and not a grand mystical creator. "Fine," the Church would probably reply, "God in his wisdom created the grey entities and they, in their turn (perhaps unbeknown to themselves), carried on the process of creation."

An interesting question is what do the ETs themselves think in regard to their own evolution? It would surely have to be a special event (since they are blessed with such high intellect) rather than some natural selection event that may apply to the flora and other fauna in their own world. A divine creative God in this sense, would certainly fit the bill, especially as it is well installed in religious doctrines in the statement that God is, was, and always will be. In this regard, God would have, in a sense, created humans. Albeit only indirectly.

Perhaps the universe itself always was and always will be. We have said in other work that even though the expansion of the universe is (strangely) increasing, it may eventually slow down and bring itself to a position where an implosive rather than explosive force may cause all the material to slowly then violently crash back in to a massive black hole which would be the 'end of days' or another violently explosive big bang, before the process starts all over again. The Vatican library has a vast collection of books, which we assume certain scholars and researchers can gain access to. Have the secrets of Fatima all been revealed? And why the refusal to reveal the last secret that was requested some years ago?

Popes are usually elected when advanced in years. It is doubtful that they would live long enough to have read every book in the faculty, even if they spent every day of their lives reading them. Will it ever be revealed that Jesus did produce an heir or not? Was there a holy bloodline? Would this be the real meaning of the 'Holy Grail', and not a cup at all? Did he marry Mary Magdalene?

Certainly, the cup of the Last Supper would not be a silver jewel-encrusted 'chalice'. Jesus, his disciples and followers, were poor and only basic utensils would have been used – most probably made of wood. It is generally felt that the Vatican does retain many secrets; perhaps they know more about our alleged Greys than we imagine we do, which is very little in terms of hard facts.

It is said that Prime Ministers and presidents, once elected, have highly secret revelations made known to them in order for them to be aware how to react to a military threat. As chief of the armed forces, they would have to make the final decision on whether or not to issue the order to release nuclear weapons on another country. President Truman had to make the decision, but not due to a threat. Rather something that had long subsided. Its assumed aim (although some say it was retribution for Pearl Harbour) was to end the war in the Pacific as soon as possible, but other major revelations would, no doubt, be revealed to a person obtaining high office. Of course, that would not necessarily mean that they could discuss them with anyone else, perhaps not even the Vice President.

We may ask, does this same process of revelations apply to a newly elected Pope? Since with having its own observatory, that there could be intelligent life elsewhere in the universe, therefore, the major event of divine creation, the Earth and everything on it, would have to shift mentally away from our own importance in the scheme of things, which of course members own of the Church themselves died for saying so in the past when suggesting the possibility of other earths and extra-terrestrial life.

When considering who it would be that took on the task of enlightening the Pope regarding profound information regarding the beings we call the Greys, it would hardly be the senior Cardinals who would do such enlightening as they in turn become Popes and would need no enlightening from them, it would have to be from another source.

Possibly, the head of the Swiss Guard who are the ones responsible for the security of the Vatican and, of course, the Pope's wellbeing. The amazing events that happened at Fatima in Portugal, were well covered in the press at the time is the story related by the three shepherd children gathered in its intensity, but it was not so much as what the three children had seen in their vision that captured the front-page headlines but rather the events of all the slaughter occurring in Europe at the time during the First World War.

Added to this, the fiercely spreading disease known as 'Spanish Flu' probably more intense than our current pandemic that at least had the benefit of intense medical research in order to combat it. The worldwide epidemic of the Spanish flu was decimating the world's population. The four horsemen of the Apocalypse were certainly in full gallop in those times.

The events concerning the three children at Fatima (one of which became a nun) had quite noticeable connotations with regard to the modern-day reports of sightings contributing to the UFO phenomena. The record of the event at Fatima in Portugal is logged in the newspapers at the time and no doubt can be accessed by researchers. One could conjecture whether the full details of the UFO aspect of the occurrence were made known to the Pope and retained as the third secret known to the girl, who later became a nun. Her name was Lucia, and she received the secrets from a 'lady of light'.

The event is recorded in the newspapers of May 13th 1917, but not necessarily on the front page, given the major events we mentioned, that were seen as much more important. However, the UFO aspect of the event is well noted. Part of the report contains the Sun coming closer to the Earth 'spinning around', changing colour and so forth. All these factors are contained in UFO reports. In any case, it is for certain that a newspaper report may differ from reliable reports of people who actually witnessed the occurrence. As the story from the children gathered momentum over the months, the audience who gathered at the specified time for an appearance amounted to twenty-five thousand people. There would no doubt have been some priests, maybe a few bishops, who witnessed the event and would have written a complete report for the Church. This probably exists among the Vatican papers.

Although the object was in the position of the Sun, the people found they could look at it without shielding their eyes and with the ease of looking at a bright full moon. If the object was a controllable disc, it had taken up a position in order to match the size of the Sun. This, in fact, occurs 'coincidentally' with regard to the Earth and the Sun. This is why we are able to observe a total eclipse. If advanced radar technology had been in place in 1917, there is no doubt that corroborating reports of a 'bogie' or blip would have been recorded in that vicinity.

One has to admire the courage of their convictions with regard to the little girls when subjected to threats as to what would happen to them if they did not admit to making up the story. They were told they could be plunged into a pot of boiling oil. The sub prefecture of the police, who made these threats to the girls, also added, "Your little brother has already been fried." The girls turned quite pale but did not recant their story. Clearly, they did not contrive the story and believed in it themselves. Just as in Biblical times, there were no other alternative explanations at hand, so it had to be seen as divine in nature, which, for all we know, it was. One of the reasons the children were chastised so severely by their mother is because the people were well aware of the event at Lourdes that had occurred some sixty years previously. As a result, children who had probably heard of it were trying to create their own 'lady of light' story.

It was Lucia, the girl who later became a nun, who stated that the 'lady of light' had revealed a certain number of secrets to her. Some of the crowd who probably responded to the reporters of the incident said that they had seen a 'ball of light' and another 'an aeroplane of light.' Aeroplanes were quite a novelty in those times, but the main point was that it was 'something moving in the air.'

Since over a hundred years have passed since the Fatima incident and with the advancement of scientific thinking, plus the acceptance of the UFO phenomena, in itself, then any extra-terrestrial connotations of the incident would not startle modern day humanity too much. Particularly when a Pope himself has also since experienced a UFO encounter. So, it would not be too impious for us to ask just what those secrets were. Some stories have appeared over the years claiming what was in them, but some turned out to be either hoaxes or what today could be called 'fake news.' It would be better to sweep away all the conjecture and clarify the situation, particularly since a Pope himself has experienced a close encounter (of the first kind).

In 1950, Pope Pius XII was treated to a celestial encounter when walking in the Vatican gardens. An account of this sighting was related to Cardinal Tedeschini, who, when speaking of it, said, "The Sovereign Pontiff was much troubled and very moved, as I have never seen him in such a way before. He honoured me with his confidence with regard to what he had seen. He told me yesterday I saw a wonder which made a great impression on me." The Cardinal then made some remark about the Pontiff, noticing some odd motions of the sun and in what form it took (another similar reference to Fatima and some similar UFO reports).

The Cardinal went on to quote the Pope and his experience, "It was October 30th 1950, two days before the anniversary of the Ascension into Heaven of the Blessed Virgin Mary. At about 4 o'clock in the afternoon, I was taking my usual walk in the gardens of the Vatican, reading my official papers, when I raised my eyes to see a phenomenon, the likes of which I had never seen before, an opaque globe that was surrounded by a bright circle of light, the globe was moving slightly, turning from left to right. The centre of the globe was moving without interruption."

The frequent mention of these globes and their similarity in movements and other factors definitely run to a pattern when analysing various UFO reports (strangely), mostly from the 1950s at the time of the Pope's encounter. It was stated that the Pontiff observed the same phenomenon again over three separate days afterwards. This account appeared in 'Fatima Espérance due Monde' by G Renault. With regard to the Pope's sighting and mentioning the ascent into Heaven of the Virgin Mary, he clearly believed (what else could he do in his position) that Jesus' ascension was also into 'Heaven', yet he did not attempt to infer any heavenly connotations to his UFO experience. Yet one cannot help noticing the few similarities of his encounter, with that of the audience at Fatima, where the crowd eventually rose to an estimated fifty thousand people. The newspaper reporters would have had a field day. Although many, it must be said, would have been entirely occupied with reporting the First World War and the rising casualties of the Spanish flu epidemic.

As said, many cases can be extracted from the UFO files that are similar to both Fatima and the Pope's account from the 1950s. Perhaps our hypothetical Greys were trying out a new form of craft for their earthly operations in the 50s era. It was a period of great alarm for the US when UFOs defied restricted air space by flying over the capital and the Whitehouse and the Pentagon, severely embarrassing the US Air Force, who seemed helpless to prevent it. They had some quick debunking to do. There was also widespread unidentified aerial activity over the UK, Italy and France. One wonders if the Vatican with regard to their astronomical interest and equipment whether they collect and correlate any reports from the Italian continent. One would think so if their own Pontiff had had a close encounter. Furthermore, whatever the object was, it made sure that he did not just observe it by one sighting, but on three further occasions afterwards. One would not expect the Pope had any problem with considering them as possible extra-terrestrial craft. It is comforting for many people to accept the Bible in its entirety and one would not want to take that away from them. But we would hope that we would not be consigned to the flames when passing on by highlighting the actions of the patriarchs and their adventures with entities, possibly from another world. In any case, the term extra-terrestrial simply means 'not of this earth' and angels from heaven would certainly qualify for the term 'extra-terrestrial'. In 'Pillars of Fire' I dealt in depth with this question and it must be said that the Bible presents itself in its own written words, as a document that could be interpreted as earthlings inter-reacting with extra-terrestrials rather than 'angels'. It is often confused by its own words. For example, Adam was supposed to be created along with the Earth and all other creatures, yet he was instructed to 'subdue and replenish the Earth', as though it was a long-neglected condition.

However, this work is not about 'Pillars of Fire', but many people must wonder how the theologians come to terms with all the questions that arise when one studies it rather than simply glossing over it, as students of theology must do. In my book Monkey Trials 2000, my main character as a youth asked his tutor in an R.E. lesson if Jesus always was, and what was he doing before he created everything. The student was severely rebuked for it. There was a time when this did happen. One just had to believe.

After the annihilation of the dinosaurs when the Earth had recovered and regenerated itself, it certainly would require much subduing and replenishing, and if Adam appeared, then he would certainly have his work cut out. Perhaps our hypothetical Greys could enlighten us on this event and if their predecessors had a hand in creating the first 'ground keeper' of the Earth. This lateness with regard to the appearance of Adam seems to be borne out by certain Islamic texts such as the Earth saying to Adam, "Oh Adam, you come to me when I have lost by freshness and my youth."

It is well known that many accept the possibility of an extra-terrestrial involvement in the appearance of humanity, which, of course, could be confirmed at a stroke if the alleged Greys do exist, but now may not be the time. It is said that certain biological and genetic indications exist in the human genome that are 'unique' and are not in any way 'inherited', but bear the hallmarks of purposeful insertion.

If this monumental and purposely directed human creation event did take place some fifty thousand years ago, not long before the human cultural evolution began, then Earth would have certainly 'lost its youth and freshness'. In fact, it would be middle-aged.

One could imagine a scene in a gentleman's club with a rather pompous chap confronting and aged retired vicar by saying, "Look here old boy, how do you people reconcile your beliefs with all these UFO reports and possible extra-terrestrials?" The old vicar may reply somewhat irritatingly, "You may not know, but we search the skies ourselves and we don't burn people anymore for believing such things, like poor old Bruno, we even agree with him there could be other world creatures in the universe."

After another gin or two the questioner might ask, "OK, but what about these creatures being on Earth right now hiding from us?" The old vicar might reply "Oh that's a step too far I think." One could imagine in this scenario the Greys grinning at each other (if they can grin) communicating with each other with something like, "They'll soon find out." As we have said, the Church has considerably modified its position today, but the fact remains that down through the ages the Church and popes have removed or altered many of the passages, texts and scriptures in the Old Testament that they viewed as unacceptable, mostly in fear of losing their power if such writings offended certain rulers, kings and emperors.

However, for all that, it is noticeable that many contradictory factors exist in the comparison of the Old Testament to the New. In the Old Testament, we are expected to accept angels as divine entities, yet their actions totally defy that description. The small matter of murdering thousands of Assyrians in their sleep who were a threat to the Hebrews, not to mention an entire Egyptian army. The Hebrews took no part in these events; they preferred to let the angels take the blame.

They were even supplied with a deadly weapon that could kill their enemies even if they just touched it. If all that was not enough, down comes Moses from the mountain with the Tablets containing the message 'thou shalt not kill', on them, as a primary directive. Does it not seem strange that these factors were not questioned by the Church or the 'Holy See' that scrutinised them?

It was said that all this scrutinising, rejecting, altercation, etc., went on right until the time that the printing presses came on the scene. We must also ask how the Church feels about the situation today. There seems to be no attempt to discuss them and the British and Foreign Bible Society do not issue any official amendments to the accounts.

How about another 'Council of Nicaea' to put these matters straight? Leaving them in the texts and ignoring them solves nothing. Do the students of theology have a policy 'read but don't question'? The fact is these points do not seem to be raised or debated in any serious manner by authorities on the scriptures. It is not clear whether Pope Pius XII made the following statement before or after his UFO encounter, but it is relevant to the points that we have just raised. In his encyclical 'Human Generis', he recommended that, "those who tried to explain and interpret the scriptures must not lose sight of the fact that the writers who imposed the scriptures borrowed from popular tradition (today we might call it literary licence) here and there, and made their own choice with regard to these documents as a result of what they felt was divine inspiration." In other words, their own opinions and what suited them.

However, this is exactly the point that we often make. How anyone can transform mass killing into 'divine inspiration' is hardly possible, but then, of course, that is not the least of it. 'Divine inspiration' descended upon Noah with commands to build his survival vessel while the rest of the world's population were to be wiped out, but the fact is, we always have to keep in mind the validity or otherwise of the written words.

However, the words have remained intact (and believed) for many centuries in all of this we cannot help but recall the words of a once popular song, "The things that you're liable to read in the Bible, ain't necessarily so." We may also recall the Biblical story of Jonah allegedly swallowed by 'a great fish', as the Bible says, but everyone else says 'a whale'. The song goes. "That he made his home in that fish's abdomen, ain't necessarily so." Certain discoveries over the centuries have not helped much, other than simply providing different accounts of old stories plus some new enlightening information. The Dead Sea scrolls are a good example. Also, an account by a French author Jean Doresse, in a book that he titled Les Livres Secrets de l'Egypte: Le Gnostique, he mentioned a manuscript that was written in Coptic text that (like the Dead Sea scrolls) was discovered in a clay jar in 1945. This account virtually turned the story of Noah and his ark on its head. If this account is to be believed, the Hebrew tradition that Noah saved his family and numerous animals from the flood is false. It says that in reality, Noah did not have to build a ship at all and that he found refuge in a 'luminous cloud' (something that we have become familiar with) and remained there until the waters subsided.

It is not surprising that many people would interpret this 'luminous cloud' as a UFO. In other words, Noah was saved by predecessors of our alleged Greys. But this isolated explanation does not explain the mass of other worldwide flood accounts. Therefore, we have to wonder how many other accidental discoveries may be made as time goes by. Particularly in the Middle East, where hiding away written accounts in clay jars seemed the fashionable thing to do. It would be the simple thing to do if wishing to hide some fraudulent documents in a cave on a goat herder's route. However, with regard to other Noah's of the world, no newly discovered manuscripts have denied their accounts. It is possible that the original Noah story spread rapidly, even though it may have been (in modern parlance) 'fake news'. Nevertheless, the scriptures all survived, and no consideration has ever arisen to alter them over the decades after the flood. The survivor's offspring, if having any imagination at all, could easily contrive such a story, but surely not worldwide. In this regard we consider the possibility that if our alleged Greys are with us, it is possible that some kind of force or telepathic pressure was applied to them who have the power to alter the texts in order to make sure that they do not do so. After all, a clear message is contained within them indicating the involvement of the greys' predecessors in the affairs of humanity in Biblical times. It was the writers of the scriptures, such as Moses, who applied the divine connotations to the 'angels'. But 'angels' may have been something entirely different and the sooner people release this, the sooner the Greys will like it. It would all help to prepare the Church and the people for any hypothetical revelations and also, more importantly, urge the Church to assist in such action.

It would seem that the Church would adapt more easily to the reality (if it became so) of the existence of the Greys. Certainly more so than the military and the politicians and the populations. The Church would most likely interpret them just as a higher power sent by God (who of course created them also) with a mission to teach and enlighten us with regard to the fact that as we are approaching the time of the 'big step off' in to the cosmos, and before that happens, we must look to our more negative behaviour patterns that we continually fail to modify. It never seems to end. As soon as one dispute is settled (usually by force), another arises. Any hypothetical Greys that may exist would obviously be considering a solution to this as a major priority before departing from the Earth.

The Church, with their uppermost conviction that the alleged Greys are also children of the creator along with humankind, would dearly like to confirm this by exploring the view that the Greys may look up to a higher presence, but their question would unavoidably cross into science and the clash between creation by a higher power just as the Greys predecessors would be or an earthly process of natural selection and whether they (the greys) had long ago solved this issue themselves.

Many people on Earth, of course, are quite happy to separate any religious connotations from our own human evolution and accept a natural selection process or even that we were once 'apes'. But this view will only prevail until the day the truth finally emerges regarding our origins. The unique qualities of creativity and high intelligence in many humans seems, generally, to be taken for granted and so few people think seriously about the implications of these gifts. The Churchmen, if ever they get the chance to ask the Greys about the ET biogenetic theory for the human, may not like the answer they receive.

We on Earth are driven by forces we have little control over such as the quest for more knowledge, the urge to explore and not only within the confines of the Earth, which is why it is inevitable that humans will eventually live and procreate on Mars and of course it will not end there. The Churchmen (and of course science) would wish to know what drives the Greys primarily in their existence, who may have achieved these goals long ago, and what their ultimate aim is, or have they achieved all their goals already?

Their answer may simply be, "Creation, and you in your turn will take on this responsibility yourselves, just as our predecessors did." This reply is received that way would certainly shock the Church to some degree, but the ultimate question, as far as we were concerned, would not have adequately been answered at that would be, "Who was the initial creator?"

There most certainly would be a major upheaval in ecclesiastical circles, if it became apparent that almost everything the Holy Book that guides them, would have to be reassessed and almost completely rewritten and their original conception of the 'angels' would change out of all proportion, to that accepted for centuries. So it can be seen that although the Churchmen would be the least disturbed by accepting the fact that the Greys may exist and be here on Earth, the follow on to that process would certainly be more disturbing for them.

However, the fact remains that a currently unidentified 'force' does exist. Whether all the conjecture will all end with a staggering conclusion with regard to the existence of the Greys and with them finally departing to the phrase 'may the force be with you', is debatable, but not so with the existence of this 'force' in the human psyche. This force is responsible for the rovers trundling around on Mars and our ultimate plans to travel much further afield.

The possibility that this force was responsible for their own existence has been well aired and will eventually be answered or perhaps revealed to us. The Church, with its comparatively recent interest in cosmology and the universe, will eventually have to merge with science at some point in the future. Although as much 'blind faith' is required to assume apes were indirectly responsible for our current activities on Mars, as that which is required to accept the genesis version of human creation, there is not a single creature on Earth that would help us explain our origins precisely.

However, the further we proceed along this road of discovery with all our conjecture and theorising, we are stepping off on the road to an ultimate 'creator' or a 'creative event' of enormous magnitude. If we accept the 'divine creator' hypothesis, we may not be satisfied by this revelation and ask 'who created him'? We cannot imagine eternity, so it is of little use trying, but we have as much trouble if we accept the religious view that 'God is, always was and always will be.' In the cloistered Catholic colleges, there is no room for 'doubting Thomases'; one must have faith and belief. But not to question goes against all natural human tendencies. If we did not possess this quality, we would indeed be existing in little more than an ape colony.

Intelligence begets intelligence, which introduces a fearsome situation. Artificial intelligence, robotics, war machines such as sophisticated drones, machines that will be self-replicating. We can envisage a fearsome future. We have said that every new invention is initially assessed for its use in the military. This is no less true of robotic machine technology such as drones and so forth. The Church may not be too interested in questioning the Greys on this issue, but modern science certainly would.

Decades ago, a French author names Paul Thomas stated, "It is possible to imagine that there exists above us an innumerable hierarchy of beings, of which the psychic level is higher than ours and may occupy a scale of values that are quite above our own comprehension." This fits in with our own assumption regarding the existence of the Greys. However, does the evolution of intelligence have a beginning? The Supreme Being, we accept as 'God', would be at the pinnacle or summit of this universal pyramid. We can speculate to our heart's content, but perhaps we have no business trying to unravel the eternal mystery of God.

With regard to the rather alarming rate of 'the rise of the machines', such artifacts would not need the protection of their assemblies that we rely on, such as special spacesuits and an adequate supply of oxygen, which would certainly start the alarm bells ringing – not only among the alleged

Greys on Earth but the hierarchy of their home planet. Humans will take these artifacts into space. With regard to the phenomenon of alleged alien abductions, the many reliable reports from people rarely mention beings operating like robots. Instead, they seem like intelligent creatures who function much like humans and can communicate in human-like fashion, albeit telepathically. This does not debar them from being 'artificial', but the indications point rather toward a biological lifeform.

If we allow our own artificial intelligence units to advance at the current rate along with robotics, we will eventually make ourselves redundant or even subservient to the machines. There is no doubt that humans will continue in their favourite pastimes, such as war, but there would be a great reduction in human casualties, which will remove a lot of resistance or opposition to the process. We could ask, did the Greys reach this highly advanced machine and robotic intelligence long ago and unlike ourselves recognised the dangers to their life forms that they had created and terminate the entire process before it became too late?

Ancient earthly teachings instructed the newly created humans (whoever the creators were) to go forth and multiply. We cannot envisage or wish for artificial self-replicating machines to do this and become out of human control. They need not be machines. The humans in the antediluvian period became out of control and had to be terminated en masse, leaving only the more finely tuned beings to go on with the process and self-replicate more of their kind.

We may ask, was the same 'cosmic' command given out to the ancient predecessors of the Greys? Both science and religion may wish to ask the alleged Greys this question. This universal command may have gone out to other sentient intelligent life forms when the dinosaurs lumbered about the Earth, but it does not seem likely that any mysterious force commanded them to proliferate worldwide, but the 'force' of life in general that included plants and even weeds in one to be reckoned with, ask any keen gardener.

However, if there is no higher intelligence on Earth that we surmise will one day provide us with great revelations, the endless speculation will prevail. In all the sermons in all the pulpits of the world, how many among all the congregation of the world ever had a member stand up and ask the preacher outright, if he could explain all the strange activity in the days of the patriarchs and their interaction with regard to the 'angels' and their advanced capabilities that could be explained by modern day technology? The 'flow' is always in one direction from the preacher to the congregation would it not be better to have, rather than a sermon, a question-and-answer session, in order to help all those struggling to believe and accept the

The Church and the Greys

teaching as divine rather than being confused by them and the contradictions in the behaviour of the angels. In my book 'Pillars of Fire', already stated I covered some of these possible questions. Divine angels would not need to descend to Earth and artificially inseminate chosen women (even if barren) by physical activity. They would simply waive an airy hand and state 'let it be so'. The offspring from these women were purposely bred for specific purposes, but the point is, the questions still remain.

The same questions could of course be asked of the Rabbis in the synagogues, even more so as the Hebrew influence dominates the Old Testament and their patriarch Moses, caused it all in the first place with his writings in Genesis and Exodus. There are frequent attempts made to remove the mystery surrounding the startling events experienced by the people in Biblical Times, such as prolific swarms of locusts, skin infections brought on by excessive insect hatching, the Nile turning blood red. Some of these things do actually happen, as do many other things that have been explained as miraculous. But the arguments are rather weak and in fact made weaker by two factors: first, the ancients were all well aware of the 'natural' occurrences, and secondly, to have them all happening conveniently when needed by the Hebrews during their desert adventures is stretching the 'coincidence' factor to the limit.

But the old scriptures do sometimes contradict themselves. For example, in the Exodus saga, written and led by Moses, with regard to the parting of the Red Sea (Exodus XIV 21), there is mention of a strong wind from the east. This wind, that was caused by God to blow all night, dried up the Red Sea at the point where they would cross. Yet further on in the texts, Moses, with the force in his 'rod', caused walls of water on each side to rise up, allowing the Hebrews to get across. The passage states, "And the waters were a wall unto them on their right and on their left." Perhaps our alleged Greys could easily explain all the odd factors to the Churchmen if they do have many revelations to give us in some hypothetical 'final end game.' If our grey beings do exist, then it means that a couple of thousand years ago, their predecessors had formidable powers if it was they who ably assisted the Hebrews by bringing into play force fields we can only guess at. This would have included defying the powers of gravity to separate the waters into two vertical walls and bringing them crashing down upon the Pharaoh's army as they fell into the trap.

And it would seem that further assistance was given to the Hebrews when slowing up the Pharaoh's army by cutting the wheels off the Egyptian chariots. It had to be some airborne aerial craft; they were obviously the lucky ones, as they did not have the transport to be drowned, as did the faster chariots in the lead.

Our alleged Greys could nod to all this if asked and simply say, "Yes it was our predecessors," but the Church would want to ask (the Christian church that is) how did this particular mass of Hebrews qualify for all this 'special treatment' when other nations in the Middle East were being killed en masse without any extra-terrestrial assistance at all?

Everyone knows (to use a colloquialism) that there is 'no love lost' between the Palestinians and the Jews, as is plain to see in Jerusalem today. It is a long-standing feud with politics interfering in the process today. And it exists also, of course, between Christians and the Muslims even today, since (and probably before) the days of the crusades.

However, the Hebrew/Arab conflict could be even older, perhaps since Abraham, the common patriarch of the Judeo/Christians and the Muslims. Abraham's wife, Sarah, was barren until the medically advanced 'knowledge' of the 'angels' took action. The Muslims trace their ancestry back to Ishmael Abraham's first son but he was born of a servant girl and according to the scriptures Sarah drove her out and she nearly died of hunger and thirst in the desert, but was said to have been saved by an 'angel'.

Perhaps our alleged Greys could throw some light on the event. However, as for the other son of Abraham Yshq (anglicised to Isaac), he is said to be the progenitor of the Hebrews. He was born to Sarah when she was long past the age of childbearing, but the 'angels' had no problems with that, with their advanced knowledge in obstetrics (and everything else) so a second son was born of Sarah.

Does the Church never consider these strange events as possibly something other than divine? It was all part of the intricate plans of the 'angels' produced by the predecessors of our now supposed Greys. The angels were created to carry out their earthly operations as hybrid creations. This could be a valid conclusion. The 'angels' had no problems of having to assist Isaac's wife with any childbearing capabilities. She produced Jacob, who in turn had many sons, who the scriptures relate had sprang the various tribes or Israel.

If the Church did get the chance to ask of the hypothetical Greys to clear up these strange events and admit their forebears were involved, it would be a long questioning session, given that there are so many of them. There are many events mentioned all through the Biblical scriptures that could be very easily interpreted as 'extra-terrestrial', or divine, depending on the way they occurred and seen under the eye of the modern-day interpreter, which the Biblical characters did not have the advantage of.

I have dealt with many of them in detail in my aforementioned book

The Church and the Greys

Pillars of Fire, and some of them cannot help but fall into the category of 'extra-terrestrial' intervention. The Church in general and certainly students of theology must certainly be aware of them.

The question of whether the Greys exist in Earth space or not, and of their possible connection to Biblical events (when beings could quite easily masquerade as 'angels'), must have been discussed within the Church. Especially considering the fact that they have brought themselves up to date with their observatory and open-minded interest in things of a cosmological nature. Many of us would like to know if any conclusions have been reached with all these factors clearly spelled out in their manual, the Bible.

We may wonder whether the Vatican and the heads of the Church of England must have had a seminar or two to discuss such matters so relative to their beliefs, more especially when we consider Pope Pius XII had his own encounter with the unexplained. The Church could choose the option we have proposed that the Greys are a higher order of intelligence and also of course God's creations themselves that could be sent to guide humanity as God's angels tried to do when issuing all those commandments through Moses.

All that would be fine, but it could not be accepted until the Church knew a lot more about the Greys and whether they sense or lookup to a higher form of intelligence themselves? Or, on the other hand, whether they have already answered the questions of their own origins? Do they accept or have they proven that a higher lifeform or power created them? If creation is to be our burden in the future, how many life forms bore this burden in the past?

If the Greys had studied and answered all the questions of their own evolution and found that they had reached their present state of advancement by 'natural selection', that may indicate that they are the first and gradually became able to create more intelligent life, we could assume, that we are the second, but as it stands, we are not aware of any other adventures and discoveries they had experienced before encountering Earth.

But the question is, why did it work so well for them when achieving all that intellect when (as they would be aware) it did not completely work for us? We still have not rid ourselves of our negative and more undesirable qualities. There must be a fear that if the Greys are not 'gods other children', the whole foundation and basic structure of the ecclesiastic organisation would crumble. If the Greys began the creation process and we eventually carry it on, then the Greys would take the place of the Church's grand creator or 'god substitute'. There would no longer be any room for an almighty grand creator. How could this be tolerated or accepted by the Church?

If the Church has considered these factors, they may be reticent to ask such questions, less they receive an unwanted reply. Of course, agnostic scientists among the anthropologists, who firmly believe in the natural selection process as being responsible for human appearance, have already confronted this issue and accepted it they would have nothing to lose but would only 'gain' by the vindication of their theory, but they could be wrong of course by formerly assuming that this had happened on Earth now it would be the 'alien creation' believers to keep their theory in vogue. This would result in everybody being happy but the Church, but for all that, even the Greys would surely not be aware of what was going on in the rest of the planets or have visited them all. So a grand creative god cannot yet be written off as not having created this vast and wondrous universe.

Even if the Greys had travelled the length of our galaxy, there are still an unaccountable number of other galaxies. When the astronomers noted what appeared to be a dark patch among the furthest stars, they trained the Hubble space telescope on this patch and it was synchronised so that even as the telescope orbited it would still remain peering at this dark patch. The results were stunning. It too was filled with stars, some estimated as ten billion light years away. They were almost looking back to the 'big bang' itself.

Even more poignant was the fact that when the black spectral lines were analysed, they showed no carbon in their emissions, indicating that they were the earliest stars in all of the creation. Surely, no visiting humanoid greys could possibly know all the secrets of creation from so far away? When humans do explore the galaxy and, in their turn, enhance the intelligence of other creatures, we would still have a vast amount to learn and may never learn it all. When we reflect on the genius of the past and present and that they only utilised a small amount of their brain material, there is still a vast amount of 'money in the bank', so to speak. Surely, one day it will come to be utilised, otherwise what is its purpose? If this does occur, super humans will exist on Earth.

If this happens, we will probably find it even harder to accept that any hominid homo erectus or Neanderthal creature has had any part in our evolution. It would seem even more unlikely that modern humans naturally 'leap frogged' over a vast period of usually snail-paced evolution. This makes it very easy to accept the ET creation hypothesis. But only the Greys could answer this question definitively.

However, no one can dismiss the Church and its root beliefs so easily, but there is nothing we can do about the extra-terrestrial connotations.

They are there plainly to see in the written scriptures of the Old and New Testaments. Two thousand years ago, when the emissary from other than Earth, we know as Jesus, clearly informed his followers of this origin by clearly stating that his kingdom (therefore he) was not of this Earth.

The Magi (plural for magicians?) witnessed the birth of Jesus. Therefore, must have received some message regarding the imminent birth. We can only guess at how. If they were magicians, did they receive some kind of 'revelation' when performing their magic rituals? In any event, they must have been instructed to look up and follow what could not possibly be a 'star' but some moving object that finally shot a beam of light down to the birth place. No one goes to a birthday party without taking a present. In their case, it was gold, frankincense and myrrh (used in perfumery). Even at the end of Jesus' amazing life and deeds, his ascension was also non-terrestrial as he rose up into a 'cloud' that received him out of their sight (the observing crowd). It would have made sense if some of his followers had continued to watch the cloud just to see what would happen to it and would surely have written of it. They knew Jesus was up there in that cloud and would surely have continued to watch it.

Clearly, the events and actions of Jesus made a long-lasting impression on many or it would not have lasted down through the centuries. Because of all the miracles and the aforesaid extra-terrestrial connection, in particular the human creation story, clearly stated by a being not of this Earth, would it be such a dramatic revelation to accept that extra-terrestrial A.K.A. 'our greys', created humanity? But it could not be avoided that some shock would be bound to be experienced.

Do the secretive group who retain all the data that they were told to release, but chose not to, know of this possibility? If they are working with the Greys, as we have already surmised, how much data has been revealed to them that we hope one day we will have revealed to us? Perhaps very little. After all, they may be happy enough to get all the technology and advanced data that we assume they are receiving as part of the deal.

However, the fact remains that if all is finally revealed, the politicians, the people and the rest of science will survive. Only the future of the religious fraternity hangs in the balance. The major question that we have covered in this and other works, that of ET biogenetic creation, is not a product of 'new age' thinking and not just in one country. It is represented in the vacillating opinions in the minds of millions of people all over the world who have took time out to contemplate the factors sustaining such an assumption, most poignant is the longevity and obvious connection and interest in the subject of ETs on Earth and their relevance with regard to humankind, but for all the words, the idea of it all seems quite fantastic, but how can we think otherwise? With so many 'signs in the sky' and the slightly disturbing pronouncement in the scriptures that said this would be so, before 'the second coming'. Not to mention, of course, the many Biblical events that suggest other worldly beings interacting with humanity in those days.

Clearly, the writers of the scriptures did not intend for this to happen, they did not wish for their writings to be interpreted in another way. Everything had a divine motivation to them. Obviously, there is a lot of enthusiasm for the hypothesis, but the real answer to the fundamental question regarding our own origins remains unanswered from all quarters – that is, from anthropology, science and in the minds of many, except perhaps for the devoutly religious.

In the final analysis, suppose our assumed Greys do just slink away and leave everything to be revealed by the secretive group, said to be working with the Greys, which is doubtful, because in the first place they probably have not been told the whole story and secondly the Greys would be avoiding their inherited responsibility from their early predecessors, then the best group to represent the people who as well as the Church and of course science, who would be anxious to find all they could about them, their purpose and involvement with humanity. Another reason for the Church to be the representatives of humanity in some 'final revelations' scenario would be the fact that the Greys would know that the basic tenets of their faith is peace, love and non-violence. So they would rather participate with them than a group of medal-adorned generals with a mass of troops behind them bristling with weapons.

Beforehand of course assuming, they had received a little forewarning, they would have some time to preach that no threat to humanity is apparent which when emphasising the long residence of 'our guests' it is clear "They mean us no harm and are also 'Gods' other children come to enlighten us", and so forth, this surely would have a great calming effect on the masses.

As people generally are intrigued by mysteries, this is another point they emphasise in that all their questions could be cleared up, but of course as we have said, the Church itself would be more than a little worried about the answers they may get relating to their own beliefs, but they would have to set that aside and mindful of calming the people.

We are assuming a lot, when we think that our Greys would know all the answers, but both science and religion would love to get some answers with regard to the Ark of the Covenant, the Turin Shroud, the Biblical events involving off Earth entities, the Biblical miracles, but most of all the real identity of Jesus.

If things proceeded well in this situation, the Church may eventually pluck up the courage to call our Greys to account for, or explain their activities (if it was true) regarding the severe measures that they took in the days of Noah, Moses and the exodus, if they really did kill newborn children and also fifty thousand Assyrians as they slept, just to help one small group of humanity to get everything they wanted. The Church may not find the courage to push things this far, but they are still valid questions that require some answers, but of course, we as humans would not be too anxious to be blamed for the actions of our parents just generations past, let alone a couple of thousand years.

They would also ask who exactly the Biblical angels were. Again, if they could find the courage, they would have to ask the final questions, "Why are you abducting humans from the Earth? What are your intentions regarding them?" We could imagine that at this point the Greys may begin to feel that humans are becoming a bit too inquisitive as this kind of information may not even have been revealed to the alleged secretive group that we assume they are working with, but they need to be answered.

Until all these hypothetical grand revelations occur (if ever), we will all just carry on wondering about such things, that the conspiracy theorists revel in, such as the Ark of the Covenant, the Turin Shroud and so forth. With regard to the latter, it seems to be a continuing saga, with assumptions due to scientific tests, that it is a fake. Then, when further scientific tests are carried out, its mystery is on the table again.

Naturally, the Church are not anxious to see it being carved up and have reluctantly allowed only snippets from the corners to be scientifically tested, then other scientists point out that such areas have been contaminated with human DNA with past handlers treating the Holy Relic with respect, have had led it gingerly mostly at the tips, invalidating past test results and so it continues, with new theories and suggestions arising all the time.

In certain TV programmes, dealing with mysteries, conspiracy theories and so forth, an interesting story arose with regard to the Turin Shroud and it was suggested that it was purposely produced by the artistic genius Leonardo Da Vinci. Curiously, if one compares pictures of Da Vinci when aged to the image on the Shroud, there is a remarkable likeness. It was stated that Da Vinci knew a wealthy family who possessed an article that they had been assured was the genuine Shroud of Christ. Da Vinci was asked if he would restore its fading images. Da Vinci recognised it as a fake straight away and told them so, adding, "If you are going to possess a fake, then you should have a more convincing one."

Da Vinci was a brilliant artist and employed many advanced techniques for his time. He also produced many works for the medical profession, showing every muscle and sinew in great detail. He had access to cadavers and carried out many dissections. He would obviously have needed the help of a trusted assistant in all of this. Da Vinci would have the Blood he had access to, daubed by his assistant on his back, to represent the scourge marks. He would then lie on his back on the cloth, keeping quite still for a while. Then he would have all the wounds of Christ daubed on the front part of his body, such as, those caused by the Crown of Thorns, the wound caused by the lance, he would cross his arms over his groin area and have the blood applied to represent the nail wounds in the hands and feet and so forth.

At this point, he was ready to have the top Shroud (laid out behind him) to be pulled over and patted firmly into place, ensuring all the wound areas would be imprinted on the cloth. He would lay there for a while, letting the blood congeal and then, 'voila', a shroud. It would then be neatly folded and placed in a casket suitable for such a Holy Relic.

While this is only theory and conjecture, it is as good as any other, at the present time. As said, the Church is not going to allow this Relic to be pulled about for this, that and the other test, so it seems it will hang onto its secrets for some time to come. One remarkable feature that stands out in quite a startling way is the negative image of the body when photographed. It is extremely lifelike.

Let us go back to the time shortly after Jesus finally expired. That is, the cessation of the life signs. His close disciples would have obtained permission from the Romans to remove the body from the Cross and taken for entombment. Someone would have to climb the ladder to get to the body of Jesus from the Cross. It would have been unlikely that they had the tools to pull out the stout nails from the Cross and the person doing the removing would have probably had to accomplish the gory task of pulling the wrist off through the nails and carrying out the same process with the feet.

The corpse (as they imagined it was) would have been modestly covered by a shroud for decency and brought down to the litter or carrying cart to be transported to the tomb. Further movements, although small, would be continually having a 'wiping' or a smudging effect on the shroud as it moved across the wounds, then when placing the body in the tomb, even more of these effects would take place.

Clearly, the end result of all this would have only resulted in a blood stained cloth. Clearly, the Turin Shroud, as we know it, is too good to be true in the sense of its artistic perfection. It would have been comparatively easy for Da Vinci to obtain cloth from the Holy Land that had been woven in the same process that had been followed for centuries. Also, he could have impregnated it with pollen and the residue of plants and foliage from the area rubbed into the cloth later. It would then be ready for future examiners to ponder over. Da Vinci would know that it would be carefully stowed away for a long time to come after it fell into the hands of the Church. This theory may be just as good as any other at the present time. When we return to the subject of the Greys, if their predecessors were active on Earth and actually carried out the advanced scientific revival process on Jesus, he would have then been free to leave the tomb (as he did) to reappear to his disciples with his wounds still apparent and later he departed from them by rising up into the air where a 'cloud' received him out of their sight.

As for the shroud that covered Jesus, it would have been removed as a bloodstained sheet and cast to one side in order that the revival process could begin, with perhaps little, if any, consideration given to its future importance.

But to return to the process of being able to converse with the Greys, again, they may be able to clear up all of these questions. It is hardly likely that a cosy 'question time' scenario could be setup, but it would be ideal if it could. The major question is how the populations of the world would, in reality, react to an actual appearance given the substantial amount of time that the 'chosen few' have withheld the facts from everyone else. The shock and panic reaction, which is an inborn fear of the unknown by the human, would not land in their lap; others would have to deal with it, the military and the National Guard, no doubt.

In this regard, the Church should be given the task of preparing the people, but of necessity, they would have to be firstly informed fully of all the background facts and data regarding the Greys and their past lengthy involvement with humankind and simply, because of this, they pose no threat to humankind. The Church would surely do a better job of accomplishing this than a group of ex-security spooks appearing who the people never trusted in the first place, to state, "Don't worry, they mean us no harm." The ecclesiastical group could ensure people of this simply by stating that they have been in contact and had obtained assurance of this fact and that they only had to sit and listen and all will be revealed. We have stressed, and it may be true, that the biggest problem of all facing the Greys and the hidden few, plus the entire scientific community would be the predicable reaction of the human, with its automatic assumption of concluding anything unknown is a threat. We have already highlighted this when we consider the remark we mentioned, made by a supposedly highly intelligent being, when stating, "We now have the technology to send ET back where he came from." This clearly assumed, without (obviously) knowing anything at all about them, that ET must naturally be a threat and is typical of many people in positions of power in the US military, with their (crudely put) 'kick ass' attitude.

This is precisely why the Church and also the religious hierarchy of all the countries of the world should be present in the forefront of preaching to the people, the most important sermon of their lives, that is how to react to the appearance of the Greys should it ever come the pass and stress the need to be calm.

In suggesting that the Church should be given the task of acting on behalf of humanity and managing the obvious trauma that would descend on the masses, we could ask 'well why not?'. After all, it was they who were deprived of the initially expected 'second coming', which was the event that the Church fully expected and that was taught by the words of St Paul himself in AD50.

However, shortly after this date, that was the fully expected time of deliverance and suppression of the wicked. All the evidence pointed toward a major postponement (or some might say 'reprieve') of the event by (planet) Heaven. This could be an equally important question that the Church could put to the Greys. They could ask why such a postponement took place after it had been spoken of so freely by their assumed emissaries on Earth that included Jesus himself as well as St Paul. Surely, it would have been a far easier task for them to accomplish in those times, when armies had no special weapons, lasers or bacteriological weapons to use against them, only spears. With the volatile behaviour of so many humans today, this is seen as strange. At that time, there must have been a major reason for such a postponement.

However, if it became clear that, what we could call a 'second coming', was imminent, then if all the formerly retained data was released to the Church, they could then formulate the most important action of their lives and prepare the people accordingly for the great sermon.

To return to the first postponement, their emissary Jesus made it clear that with the exception of 'planet heaven', no one else on Earth knew when it could occur, "No not even the angels themselves, but only my father in heaven." But Jesus did make it clear that, "This generation shall not pass until all these things are fulfilled."

Jesus is estimated to have been crucified about AD 30 to 35. Some fifteen years later, St Paul was writing to the Thessalonians, "We which are alive and remain, shall be caught up with them in the clouds (UFOs under cover?) to meet the Lord 'in the air'. You all know well that the day of the Lord cometh." Even when Paul was beheaded, he still had faith that the culmination was at hand and that he was merely preceding his companions to heaven by a short time. Eventually, those who considered themselves as the righteous begin to complain and speak of false prophets and asked, "Did not this seductor faithfully promise that he would himself return in a 'chariot of fire' in the clouds at the same time, and that we would all be changed into citizens of the kingdom that is 'not of this world'?"

The celestial or extra-terrestrial connotations in all of this written data are plainly obvious. As the expected event did not happen, the imaginary ecclesiastical audience in our aforementioned contrived 'question time' scenario could ask of the Greys. Why? After all, it caused much embarrassment to their other emissaries left on Earth who had to bear the brunt of all the negative reaction and disappointment and all the anger over 'false prophets'. The majority of the anger, of course, was among the Hebrews, who had suffered under the Roman oppression for so long and hoped for a return to smite their enemies and take them off to heaven. It cannot be avoided that when one reads of all these events, particularly in the Old Testament, that the extra-terrestrials or alleged Greys have many questions to answer today.

It seems that when reading of these events, that the Disciples, patriarchs and the prophets, many of whom later became saints, were quite aware that they were dealing with creatures who were 'not of this Earth', even if they did accept them as 'angels'. For example (when referring to the second coming), "Then shall appear the sign of the son of man in the heavens, coming in the clouds with great power and glory."

For those who accept the possibility that Jesus was a very special cosmic being that was proven by his own actions on Earth and especially his dramatic departure off the Earth into a cloud, that Jesus was 'extra-terrestrial' as some members of the Church must have considered. They could surely have this confirmed, along with answers to the many other questions they would ask if it was allowed to happen. The whole operation regarding the 'plan Jesus' was that a great example should be shown to mankind not to slip back into their 'ancient nature' and obey the directives the predecessors gave to Moses for human behaviour. Surely, such high intelligence and creativity would be wasted on humankind if they could not shed their savagery. Jesus certainly could have saved himself, but that was not part of the plan. He simply kept silent, which infuriated Pontius Pilot, who it seems, did his best to save him. He needed a crime and it could not be proven that Jesus had committed one, or even that he spoke out about the Roman Oppression. This could be one reason why the Jews turned against him, rather than supported him. He was leaving without having freed them. They had expected great things from Jesus, but all they got was words. They knew about the miracles that he had achieved, but the miracle they wanted was the destruction of the occupiers. They looked more toward Barabbas in this regard, which is no doubt why he escaped crucifixion. However, Jesus did not.

The Romans had installed Herod Antipas as the King of the Jews, but Herod was not in fact a Jew, he was of the Bedouin tribe. He could not tolerate another being coming along, who the people referred to as King of the Jews. Nevertheless, he did give Jesus the opportunity to display his miraculous powers in front of him and his courtiers, but as said, this was not part of the plan.

The very successful production by Tim Rice and Andrew Lloyd Webber Jesus Christ Superstar was initially condemned as blasphemous even by those who had not seen it. However, it was far from that. It summed up the attitude of the people and the power of the time. Herod said, "Jesus, I am overjoyed to meet you face to face. You are all we talk about, all around the place, healing cripples, raising from the dead." After gasps from his courtiers, he adds, "at least that's what they said." He then suggests to Jesus, "If you are the Christ, the great Jesus Christ, prove to us that you are no fool. Walk across my swimming pool. If you do that for me, I'll let you go free, c'mon King of the Jews!" Jesus must have been quite tempted, but his will and determination had been shorn up when he wavered in the Garden of Gethsemane he asked of 'God the Father', "Surely I have done enough, if possible let this cup (the crucifixion) pass from me." If it came to pass that the Church really did have the chance to calm the people and prepare them for the final revelations by the Greys, the Churchmen would hardly know where to start.

Obviously, starting from the beginning, the Greys' part (if any) in the appearance of humanity would surely be top of the list. Second, whether they were actively engaged in the Biblical flood during Noah's time, and of course, thirdly, whether they had any hand in the other Ark and its fearsome capabilities. They may also ask of its current whereabouts – although it is doubtful that this would be revealed given the proclivity of the military to utilise such items in war and conflict.

The Churchmen may have it explained to them that their predecessors had to take very stern measures due to the fact that so many humans had slipped back to their 'ancient nature.' They may also make it clear that their forebears had given humans the necessary brainpower and intellect to deal with current human mental aberrations; for example with through the advancements in neurology, in studies of stem cell research, and by laying bare all the human genome. Moreover, humans can now also deal with these issues themselves through gene therapy.

Today, geneticists themselves have been astonished at the advancements and discoveries happening in the field of genetics; all the secrets of human unacceptable behaviour will be revealed and must be eliminated in the appropriate manner or there may be little future for mankind as currently there is no sign of all those spears becoming 'plough shares.' This was predicted in the ecclesiastical 'second coming.' We have to ask, how would it come about with its equivalent involving the Greys? It is easy to speak of 'genetic manipulation,' but it is bound to be more complicated than that. We cannot envisage a situation where the faulty gene would simply be snipped out of the double helix and that that would solve the problem. There are probably groups of genes working together and in unison with each other that control various aspects of human behaviour.

Perhaps Jesus himself may have been referring to this issue when he stated, "The tares and the good seed are so entangled in us that it is impossible to tear out the one without tearing out the other." This is interesting in the sense that if we assign an extra-terrestrial attachment to the Biblical events, in particular to Jesus himself, then this may reflect that the forerunners of the Greys achieved everything except full control of the human genome. They didn't at that time succeed in eliminating the more basic instincts that are still apparent in humans today – the instincts that cause all the negativity, mental turmoil, crime, and warlike behaviour.

But of course, a long time has passed since then and the Greys would no doubt have no problem in dealing with these problems today (if we were to agree to it). But this may not be necessary if we refer back to the point that neuroscientists are "… astonished by what we are achieving" (in the field of genetic research). This seems to indicate that it can be done and everything is possible with regard to the elimination of negative human behaviour. That problem is that the negative forces are so strong that certain humans may not allow it to happen. Military control could prevail by restraining the geneticists from eliminating the necessary aggression required from soldiers in war and reducing future generations to weak saintly individuals. Any hypothetical Greys among us would, of course, be quite aware of this. This problem is reflected in the Biblical teachings of the fight between good and evil – or between the 'redeemer' and the 'antichrist'. We can therefore recognise an analogy here. But how do we determine the good and the evil? Does the answer lie in the forces of the human brain? The geneticists could be described as the good, and the undesirable influences in the brain as the evil. Or, evil could be interpreted as the military forces and their intention to "send ET back where he came from," and/or, the desire to carry on manufacturing killing equipment while defeating any attempt to remove the undesirable mental qualities that desire the continuation of killing. Instead of the dramatic circumstances of mass human annihilation to solve the problem of human 'evil' (as may have occurred in the ancient past), today, science will be the 'redeemer'.

However, in the days of Noah, a few men were found that perhaps could be utilised to what we might call 'genetically cleanse' future generations. These unique individuals must have been sought out all over the world and not just in the story of Noah and his Ark. There were many other 'Noah's' with their own specific instructions to select other beings fit to be saved and, of course, as many other creatures as possible. We have to ask, if the clergymen did partake in a session with the alleged Greys as 'go-betweens' or representative of humanity, how would they broach the subject of the Biblical annihilations that were formerly accepted as the wrath of God? Would the Greys comment on them? Plainly, it was their forebears who were attempting to eliminate the mistakes they made during the human creation programme. Almost certainly, the Church would ask about the subject of the ascension of Jesus in a 'cloud' (and also later that of his own mother) and his revival process.

The author, Paul Thomas, who has highlights certain extra-terrestrial events in the Bible, refers to documentation alluding to the ascension of Mary. After the departure of Jesus, Mary was looked after by the friends of Jesus, particularly John, who took her, it is said, to Ephesus, where she ended her days. Then, when her time came, she expired gently. Later, presumably, after her ascension that they had not witnessed, her disciples entered the room in order to carry away her body. There was no sign of Mary.

The bed bore the marks of her body but was empty. This data was included in what the author referred to as "the definition of the dogma of the assumption of the Virgin." Paul Thomas also spoke of another enigma, the Turin Shroud. If the image on the shroud was simply painted on the sheet, then the paint should have penetrated the fibres of the material more deeply. In addition to this, it appeared that the Shroud had been subjected to a strong electrical force, not only from the outside but also from within, suggesting that a recently expired body, when wrapped in the shroud, was radiating energy. Other science-fiction-like suggestions emerged, for example, suggesting that ET carrying out a revival procedure. An experiment was carried out in a TV programme that showed that if this procedure was carried out, energy did actually transfer an image onto a cloth. It is often said that extraordinary claims require extraordinary explanations and no doubt, other theories will follow. Another factor that hints at the presence of extra-terrestrials in Biblical times, are the actual paintings of a religious nature that clearly show what could not be anything else than UFOs. These paintings even depict 'discs' – the archetypal 'flying saucer shape' – in the background.

However, the crucifixion of Jesus would be the one topic that we assume the religious assembly would wish to ask, "Was Jesus a divine entity or an emissary of your predecessors?" The answer may shake the ecclesiastical assembly, but it would have to be asked, as it is pivotal to the core beliefs of the Church. Even at the crucifixion, there was a rather dramatic event that took place with the darkening of the skies, torrential rain, and severe thunderclaps. It was traumatic enough to make one of the Roman guards declare, "Truly, this was the son of God." We have no way of knowing if this is true or not. Any of the scribes, when writing of the event, could have included this in order to reinforce the 'divine' aspect of the event.

For all we know, the Church may not have to ask as many questions as we might suppose of the Greys. A recent programme highlighted an excavation below the Vatican Archives where unusual skulls were found that looked more alien than human. If this had been investigated thoroughly, and it was shown that their evolution did occur by a form of natural selection, then how would the Church handle this dilemma? If the Greys, before allegedly arriving on Earth, had not discovered any other intelligent life forms on their planetary travels, then they would perhaps assume that they were the first. But they would still be following some cosmic laws or instructions to nurture and develop creatively intelligent beings. It would be simply something they felt because, firstly, they had the intelligence to do it, and secondly, out of concern for a species who would benefit greatly from their assistance and go forth, multiply, create and eventually reach a stage where humankind would become almost quite comparable to their own and could continue the process.

But where would this leave the Church? The theory of their own, that extra-terrestrials are all 'God's children', would be on shaky ground. However, the universe is so vast that it would be extremely unlikely that our hypothetical Greys would understand it all and certainly they would be unaware of all the processes going on with regard to every planet in a favourable position around a 'sun like' star, of which there are a great multitude.

And so, there may be questions that, although the Church felt compelled to ask, they may not like to hear the answers. If every startling event in the Biblical Holy Scriptures was based on extra-terrestrial events that were misconstrued by the patriarchs in their wonderment (such as the angels descending on their 'pillars of fire'), what would be the future of the Church and its established foundations? They must have considered these points. The only trump card to hold on to would be to ask, "Who else could be responsible for the amazing secrets of life, creation, and the unfathomable universe?" Surely, the pinnacle of it all would be in the form of a divine creator. Cold atheistic science may refute it, but what else would the Church have to cling to?

If all of this did come to pass and humans did not react violently against the alleged Greys, then they would no longer be 'alleged', but a reality. The sciences, the Church, the people, would all be fully enlightened as to their origins and science would simply continue their cosmic ambitions without the need for any wonderment with regard to the postulations of extra-terrestrials existing. As for the Seti Programme, it would continue with the belief that there must be other life forms to discover and other profound information to attain about the universe.

But what of the Greys themselves? Before their mission was deemed to be complete, they would have to insist that a protective 'ring fence' would have to be set up to ensure that the vital part of their mission was fulfilled. This would be set up by a (fully protected) human group who would carry on with their project of eliminating negative factors in the brain through genetics, whilst protected from the 'hawks' that always exist in any military organisation, who would resist it.

However, with regard to science and many of the ecclesiastical fraternity, the final answers would be required from the Greys, which is to explain their lengthy programme of human abductions. This we will deal with in the next chapter. That the mission of the Greys may be completed could be indicated by a strange occurrence reportedly of an unexplained long cigar shaped craft that had entered our solar system. Is this the craft, which must be from elsewhere in the galaxy, the great mother ship to take them home?

A recent TV programme brought up this issue. It was stated that a huge object is orbiting the Earth, not obviously noticeable from Earth. It was photographed in orbit and, as said, it had been ascertained as having emanated from outside our solar system. It may not have been the first visit and was conveniently used for the analysis of the alleged abduction

The Church and the Greys

victims, picked from their cars. A few of the most high-profile cases will be related in The Abductions and the Greys.

This large craft was first observed and photographed in 1998. It is also alleged to be the 'storage unit' where all the medical samples, blood, tissue, human/hybrid foetuses are stored. This may be the explanation for all the 'phantom pregnancies' reported that are put down to physiological factors due to the desire for a child, but possibly nurtured and removed by the ETs? Although it was photographed, it was said that NASA clamped down on the release of the photos. The choice of this alleged craft of a polar orbit would have been a good choice to observe the entire Earth's surface as it rotated. The ex-Canadian Minister of Defence was mentioned and apparently spoke of this craft as belonging to the 'Federation of Nine', who are allegedly responsible for overseeing all intelligent life discovered (or created) in the universe and they apparently have a prime directive which is, 'don't appear, don't interfere.'

If this is so, then our alleged Greys have long invalidated the order both by being seen, as well as via their alleged abduction programme. Of course, this directive could be interpreted as once a species begins its higher development (possibly due to outside creative means), do not interfere. As for the abductions, the Greys may not see it as 'interference', but simply a progress check on human development.

With regard to the secretive group who may already have all this information, it must include many scientists as well as ex CIA, FBI, and National Defence Agency people. But the scientists in the general community may not have been brought into this secretive group because of their many and varied opinions with regard to the UFO and abduction issue.

Many will agree that to deny that intelligence could exist elsewhere in the universe is preposterous, but find it a very big step to take to accept that they may be here on Earth. Indeed, many still trot out the same explanations put forth decades ago, such as mass hallucinations, vivid dreams (with regard to the abductions) natural phenomena, meteors, balloons and even refer to what they call 'the Spielberg effect.' They have a point to some degree, anyone who has observed a high-altitude weather balloon moving fast in an upper air current, or a slow-moving meteor, travelling into our atmosphere in a 'follow on' motion, matching, almost, Earth's orbital speed then moving as a yellow fireball, or a satellite could very easily be convinced they had seen a UFO.

However, the fact is that there are far too many 'close encounter' cases to rely on those explanations. To return to the information given by Paul Helyar, many people would be a bit concerned that a man could reach such a responsible position as a Defence Minister, yet could make such statements that could indicate that he may be 'certifiable'. This, however, maybe a little unfair and this situation is comparable to a character in my book The Second Coming. A senior army officer (later vindicated) was incarcerated after reporting that he had observed a Senior General communicating with a holographic image of an ET that he had witnessed. He took it to the top, but was confined to a mental institution.

However, to conclude this section, it is quite clear that something quite profound in nature is being withheld from the general public up to the highest levels, and that this must at some point culminate in a form of final revelations. These revelations will be more severe in terms of 'cultural shock' because of the stupid policy of secrecy that has thus far prevailed, instead of introducing people gradually to these matters. When the time comes, the secretive group of humans should go to Church and in a sense 'confess their sins' and reveal all. The Church should then be the ones to reveal it all to the public and explain the great advantages (and not dire consequences) of the revelations and what they mean for our future.

CHAPTER III

ABDUCTIONS AND THE GREYS

Contrary to what some people believe, the alleged abductions by extraterrestrial entities are not completely ignored by science, specifically medical science. It is also quite certain that the various security organisations do not ignore it, they would not dare. Such an important issue must be addressed, which is no doubt taking place within the security groups who also deal with the UFO phenomena.

Of course, the general public has no business enquiring about how much they may know or have discovered. We have 'no need to know', and that goes not only for ordinary people but also for presidents and prime ministers. But it is not possible to side-line such an important issue. The sheer volume of abduction claims throughout the world, and encounters of the first, second and third kinds involving what are claimed to be extraterrestrial craft, makes it impossible to side-line. It could be assumed that all of these well-documented accounts have very sinister implications. This is only one view but a natural one when considering the human mindset. As for the authenticity of the abduction issue, when two former secretary-generals of the UN are linked to the phenomenon, then we have to sit up and take notice – especially as one of them actually witnessed (along with the two security agents) an abduction occurring before their eyes.

With regard to the abduction phenomenon, many people had their interest generated (including one of the UN Secretary Generals mentioned) by the most compelling case by far, which was the Betty and Barney

Hill affair of the 1960s. Certain scientists and members of the medical profession have made appearances on TV programmes dealing with the alleged abductions and the medical procedures that were allegedly carried out by alien entities on both male and female 'victims'. The later analysis carried out on the victims in order to recall these events has often involved hypnotherapy. This does not apply to every alleged victim but only to those who are lucky enough to have their case highlighted (or who can afford it), because hypnotherapy sessions do not come cheap. Most cases follow a similar patter with many similar aspects occurring in each case. The most highlighted factor is the so-called 'missing time period' – usually a couple of hours go by during the abduction that the victims cannot account for. This is characterised as a form of amnesia.

Hypnotherapy is applied in an attempt to lift the veil of this amnesia and to uncover what exactly happened during this unexplained couple of hours. One other common factor in all cases involves the removal of cellular material of a reproductive nature as well as the taking of blood – which we know about because of puncture marks left on the victims' bodies.

Sometimes, after X-ray processes on certain parts of the body that the subject has drawn attention to, strange small 'items or implants' are evident, which are then surgically removed. But on victims who may not have had the benefit of this close attention, they may be carrying around these implants without being aware of it. A certain Dr Roger Leir, who specialises in identifying these objects and surgically removing them, has stated that thus far he has collected sixteen of these objects from various parts of the body of the victims.

Strangely, as would be expected under normal circumstances, one would expect signs of inflammation or some indications of the body's natural defences to be attempting to reject such items. We can speak clinically and objectively of these events, but just to contemplate the idea that creatures not of this Earth have arrived here from a vast distance away and removed some of its citizens for analysis, is a rather frightening and monumental phenomenon to contemplate or accept. But, the evidence in support of it is clear. Oddly, some victims, once having the items removed, have stated that they sense a feeling of relief, like suddenly having a great responsibility removed from their being; rather like freedom from something they could not define.

It seems to indicate that these items were purposely inserted for control in case the alleged Greys wished to find them again. In at least one case of an ET abduction, the perpetrators, in answer to the victim's question, stated that they could easily find them again if they wished. Some abduction victims even claimed that they had been taken more than once. Careful vetting of those who claim to have had these experiences is required, as there are always those who have a proclivity for fame and attention among the population and crave publicity. As far as I am aware, no special team has ever been trained for this and can only use their own intelligence and common sense.

We have said that if one discounts the most high-profile abduction claim of all, that is the aforementioned Betty and Barney Hill case, then it is unlikely one could believe any other claims. Even the highly qualified Dr Benjamin Simon could not accept any other explanation other than that it was simply a shared dream. However, all the factors of the case seemed to refute this.

To dream, one must go the sleep and sleeping was the last thing on their minds. They were anxious to get home as soon. Their alleged UFO encounter frightened Barney more than Betty, and he was anxious to leave the area as quickly as possible. Some human victims must be found to be more interesting than others in certain areas, which may be the reason for the implants and knowing where to locate the victims. One example would be someone like Albert Einstein; his brain was said, after analysis, to be 'wired' differently from others. He would certainly have been a subject that 'they' would have wished to re-examine. Perhaps the alleged abductors or Greys operate within a strict schedule, as the missing time always seemed to be around two hours. However, a noticeable exception was Travis Walton, who was missing for a number of days (to be mentioned later).

When the aforementioned Dr Roger Leir had the items he had removed from the victims, sent for analysis, it was found that they were 'meteoric' in makeup. That is, composed of all the minerals that are assembled in meteorites. Meteorites are often iron based in their makeup, which would be useful to detect their previous victims. Meteorites each have their own geochemical signature within its material and could be used to categorise the victims of the alleged abductions.

Actually, being meteoric in makeup strengthens the possibility that they are purposeful insertions because the only other way a fragment of a meteorite could pierce the body would be to enter it like a bullet or piece of shrapnel, which could not happen unnoticed. A burn hole in the clothing, a sharp stabbing pain, inflammation, and so forth. Nor is it likely that these items were ingested during normal food intake, as they would simply pass through the body in the normal process of human waste disposal.

But of course, all of this does not mean necessarily that the surgeons and scientists involved in these removal processes accept the ET hypothesis.

They merely presented their findings and leave the hypothesising to others. Some scientists, however, are quite prepared to accept the ET hypothesis – due to the huge numbers of worldwide claims and the patterns by which they are characterised as well as the intensive interviews with numerous victims.

One such person who is persuaded that the issue is a real phenomenon is Dr David Jacobs, who has written books on the subject. He has highlighted the convincing factors and points out the worldwide aspect of it all. Another well-qualified gentleman by the name of Dr John E Mack who was a Pulitzer-prize winner of US Harvard University was moved to accept the validity of the phenomena after being a sceptic. When realising that the abduction claims ran into their hundreds of thousands, he stated, "This is much more than an oddity, it is an epidemic." The process he went through in changing his view from sceptic to believer mirrors the case of Dr J. Allen Hynek.

Dr Hynek, in a sense, was 'used' when the US Air Force wished to portray that science had been consulted and had confirmed that there was nothing for the public to be alarmed about. The US were terrified of the possibility that they might have to admit that they had no defence against the high capabilities of the perpetrators of the phenomenon. And they were well aware of the volatile nature of the masses and their tendency to panic, and this also applied to other countries who were just as perplexed by the phenomenon. The top defence chiefs in the UK were just as alarmed as those in the US – especially considering that UFOs could fly over places such as the Pentagon with impunity.

Dr Hynek was happy to oblige when the US Air Force first consulted him. Being a sceptic and somewhat irritated by the phenomenon, he welcomed the opportunity to research and analyse it for himself. His brief with regard to 'Operation Blue Book' was primarily to present 'an air', of 'scientific rebuttal' of the phenomena. However, he did not agree to this unscientific and deceitful means of trying to fool the public. One example that he gave was that of an observer reporting a fast-moving silver disc-shaped object moving at high altitude and making abrupt changes of direction, at which the interviewer would reply, "but what was the 'main' direction of this weather balloon?"

Although this section is primarily intended to deal with the abduction phenomena, the UFO issue is inextricably linked within it and cannot be avoided. Over the years, Dr Hynek, just like Dr John Mack, changed his mind considerably with regard to the UFO phenomena and the abduction issue. Dr Hynek became closely involved in the aforementioned Betty and

Barney Hill case, even at one point sitting in on a hypnotherapy session by Dr Benjamin Simon and Barney when he was under deep hypnosis.

It is notable with regard to the individuals who have experienced abduction trauma that they do not run to a pattern with regard to their character profiles. As a matter of fact, our alleged Greys can be quite selective in their choice of their 'victims'. Even policemen are not exempt. In fact, they are quite vulnerable when on night patrol, when few people or other vehicles are about.

It was around 3:00am when a police patrolman named as Herb Schirmer on duty in Nebraska, as he was cruising along the highway, he spotted what he first thought was a truck that had broken down. One can only imagine his shock when he observed the vehicle rise up before him with flashing lights around its rim or perimeter. It was obviously a disc shaped craft. Although in shock, he managed to record what he had witnessed, including the necessary times and dates.

The worst, but most common feature, of these cases is the 'missing time syndrome.' Although the victim cannot recall any details, they know somehow that they were affected by something unexplainable and often disturbing enough to affect their health. It is better in these cases when they do not bottle it up, but talk about it with others. This way, someone can make a helpful suggestion. In the case of Officer Schirmer, a friend of his arranged for him to be subject to a regressive hypnosis. It was during this process that the complete details of his encounter emerged.

We have suggested, and it is probably true, that many victims of an abduction event may not have been given the opportunity or been able to take advantages of these processes and have done their best to push it all out of their minds and just tolerate any disturbing dreams. After all, one can have disturbing dreams without having been abducted, but the point we are making is what is the true figure with regard to the abduction events? No one knows.

In the case of Officer Schirmer, his memory returned, and he began to relate all the previously omitted additional data. Before encountering the vehicle, he originally thought was a truck. He recalls observing it actually landing in front of him. Before settling on the ground, it extended some kind of landing apparatus, or support gear, with red lights at the tips. This is interesting and it will be noted as the same description that the Hills gave with regard to their craft before they were taken aboard it.

Officer Schirmer recalled trying to start his patrol car in an attempt to escape, knowing that the craft was not an earthly machine. Whatever power the alleged ETs used to affect the minds of the victims must be extremely powerful and they must be able to implement it without being up close to their chosen victim.

In the case of Betty and Barney Hill, they were affected from above. The ETs actually took control of Barney's mind and car, causing him to turn off the main route he was on, which he had not intended to do, and which brought him closer to where their craft had landed. In the case of Officer Schirmer, he recalls trying to start his car in an attempt to escape when he saw the object landing ahead of him. It seems logical to assume that the Greys purposely singled out their victims, knowing that the highway was devoid of traffic. It's likely that the examination and medical procedures would not have taken place with their craft still sitting on the ground where they could be interrupted by a trucker on the road. They would almost certainly have left the ground, then returned the officer to the same place from where they had abducted him.

Officer Schirmer, speaking clearly, and describing in detail what had happened, related that he was immobilised, "I am prevented ... Something in my mind ... I want to get away ... They are coming out ... approaching me ... it can't be ... I'm trying to draw my revolver ... the being is holding up an object ... Paralysed ... Passing out ... It's all black." With regard to the Greys, the salient points that all run to a pattern all appeared in the case. The shortness is stature, the large controlling eyes, a 'slit' in place of a mouth, a form of telepathic communication. Under hypnosis, Schirmer stated, "It's through my mind ... Somehow ... He is telling me things, the voice is like ... broken English ..."

The reader should note all these points, as it will be shown that they appear in the same form in the most high-profile case that we mentioned and which will be related later. Naturally, it will be assumed that Officer Schirmer read of the abduction claims and simply dreamt it all. Police officers are far too busy to be dreaming they have to check in, make reports, they cannot fall asleep in their cars. It should be noted that Officer Schirmer underwent a polygraph test that he volunteered for and it showed no indications other than Schirmer was telling the truth. It could be assumed that with the respective features in most of these cases, is that the greys may have standard operating procedures that they follow in each case. Entire books have been written about the intricate details and some rather astounding claims that may reflect an alien agenda. Not many people have considered the one that may reveal the real purpose of their abduction programme.

However, the following case just seems to run to the usual pattern, although no less traumatic for the abductee and again, certain procedures will be noted when we consider the final case. The author Raymond Fowler wrote of the 'Andreasson Affair'. Again, hypnotic regression procedures were applied to the abductee in order to elicit the various details of her experience.

This lady claimed that she was removed from her home at night in Massachusetts. She was immobilised by small humanoid creatures (who else but the Greys) and was rendered semi-conscious. It would be interesting to consider that if ever a conclusion to the whole affair did happen with an actual appearance on Earth, many thousands of people would recognise them like they would with meeting old friends on the street, but not necessarily with the same reaction.

Betty Andreasson, under hypnosis, revealed the now familiar details. The large eyes, the greyish pallor, the slit for a mouth, the thin limbs and so forth. In her hypnotic condition, she relates that she was "Immobilised, I can't move ... I can't do anything ... I'm not afraid of him." It seems that the Greys have this power to remove any fear from the subjects in order, no doubt, to make them easier to handle. Betty Andreasson goes on ... "Says he won't hurt me." She then describes her test procedures in quite a detailed fashion: "An examination room ... some complicated instruments ... I'm on a block ... lights coming from the walls ... Wires and needles ... They are inserting a long silver thing into my belly button" [note this for when we come to the Betty and Barney Hill case] ... They tell me there are some parts missing." This is an interesting point because Betty Andreasson had experienced a hysterectomy, but it shows clearly that the perpetrators were quite familiar with the human female anatomy.

There is no reason why they should not be. Betty Hill was subjected to the same procedure regarding a needle into her navel. In her case, the Greys were removing eggs from her. They must have improved their procedure in this as Betty Andreasson did not mention pain during this process, but Betty Hill certainly did and she let them know about it vocally.

The eggs, the reproductive material removed from the Hills, may have occurred in all the other cases, who have not had the opportunity of bringing their case to light and may well indicate something quite profound is happening as we have touched upon in the first chapter of this book. For these operations to have gone on for so long, implies that the Greys are not merely curious about human anatomy (they are clearly well familiar with it by now) but that there must be another purpose.

Some abduction claims seem to stray into the realms of science fiction, but may nevertheless be true. These are always cases involving females. Many have reported seeing foetuses floating in bluish liquid and some have claimed to have been re-abducted and then 'bonded' with a kind of hybrid child that they somehow knew was partly their own. These accounts certainly stretch the credibility factor. For example, if the Greys, during the routine abductions, are so careful with what they reveal, why would they allow a secret reproductive human/hybrid operation?

One of the most amazing cases connected to the abduction phenomenon was to do with a report of the observation of small beings transporting a female victim out of the window of her high-rise apartment block. Before we too quickly assign this to the science fiction category, we would add that this event was actually witnessed by the current (at that time) United Nations Secretary General Javier Pérez de Cuéllar, who was accompanied by two security guards. This amazing event took place in Manhattan in the US on November 30th, 1989.

In John G Fuller's book The Interrupted Journey, he says, "The greatest mystery about the abduction experience is that any assumption on the basis of the material revealed is hard to conceive or understand. An abduction by humanoid intelligent beings from another planet in a spacecraft has always belonged to science fiction. To concoct a story of this magnitude (the Betty and Barney Hill case) would require an inconceivable skill and collaborative capacity for ordinary folk. It is hard for the Hills to accept that their abduction actually took place as it is for any other intelligent person to accept. In fact, the attitude of the Hills is, 'We did not expect or look for the event to take place.' In fact, Barney resisted it and continually wished to deny its existence. He always said, 'We didn't know what happened in the missing two hours until we heard our own voices on the tapes. It was as difficult to believe for us as it would be for anyone else. We only knew that after all the pieces began coming together. Our conviction grew on us that the experience did actually happen.'" The Hills' experiences were recorded separately over various sessions by a highly respected and qualified Boston hypnotherapist, Dr Benjamin Simon, who, during World War II, specialised in dealing with traumatised troops with the condition or affliction commonly known as 'shell shock.' Simon had wide experience in dealing with such cases that were common among traumatised soldiers removed from the heat of battle. But to return to the wide variety of abduction claims, the event we formerly referred to took place, as said, in Manhattan involving the UN Secretary Javier Pérez de Cuéllar. This information came out only later, perhaps due to the meagre amount of data released by the secretive group who decided what the rest of us will see, by pretending to comply with The Freedom of Information Act.

However, there is no doubt that right from the start, this event would have been highly classified as de Cuéllar was accompanied by two security agents and they would be well attuned to the procedure. The three people in the vehicle actually witnessed a woman along with a few alien entities moving up in a bluish beam of light to a UFO hovering above the apartment block from which she was taken.

If all that was not strange enough, why, after all the attempts by the Greys to remain hidden, subdue the abduction victims, take steps to obliterate their memory, and then appear without any fear of being observed? In a busy city like Manhattan, although there is a lot of traffic and there are many people about, the plain fact is that during everyday life, very few people actually look up unless they are distracted by a flash or a noise of any kind.

The obvious indifference shown in this case by the Greys could indicate that they care little about being seen from time to time, as it will help to attune the human mind in general to the idea that they do actually exist on Earth. And this would help to ease the trauma of the final 'revelations' scenario. After this event, Javier Pérez de Cuéllar, although possibly warned about the consequences, would have been very anxious to confide in someone, as it would have been very traumatic for him. De Cuéllar would have found it a difficult observation to keep to himself and would certainly have felt that something so profound ought to be announced in the UN Assembly to enlighten the world to what was happening on Earth. There was a procedure that he could have followed and that is, since the UFO phenomena and the abductions were already known of worldwide, he could have suggested that all the countries of the world should offer their best brains and expertise to a worldwide investigative study of this phenomenon.

As well as Javier Pérez de Cuéllar, another previously appointed UN Secretary General, U-Thant, would certainly agree with this proposition as he himself had become quite interested in the abduction issue when he heard about the high-profile Betty and Barney Hill case. He and Javier Pérez de Cuéllar would have made a formidable pair and could have instigated a more intensive investigation than that which occurred in Project Blue Book or the later Condon Report. Both of which were rather sceptic-ridden and un-intensive from the start. The Secretary General U Thant had no doubt read of the high-profile Betty and Barney abduction claim in John G Fuller's book, The Interrupted Journey, which gave a very detailed account of their experiences.

The expert on the UFO issue Dr J Allen Hynek was also aware of, and took interest in the Hills' case and, at one point, was able to listen to the compelling tape recordings that were taken by Dr Simon. Dr Simon, who took on the Hills' case, was initially only interested in their amnesia.

Apparently, the outline of the Hills' story had been published in Look magazine and U Thant, the UN Director General, after reading the account, noted that there were a good deal of similarities to cases of abduction that had been reported by many member nations of the UN.

U Thant, being aware of John G Fuller's book, which was a concise account of the Betty and Barney Hill case, and of Dr J Allen Hynek's interest in the abduction phenomena, contacted them and expressed his wish to meet both of them in his New York office. U Thant knew that Dr Hynek would acquaint him on the subject and could no doubt answer his many questions. U Thant was primarily interested in the general public's reaction to the phenomenon. We have said that there exists a certain selective group who act above the law with regard to The Freedom of Information decree and do this by blanking out most of the texts on the items they do release. Dr Hynek covered this point with U Thant, who agreed with him. In particular, it was Hynek's wish that serious intelligent research into both the UFO phenomenon and the alleged abductions was imperative.

Since Presidents have made remarks such as, "Nobody has told me and I want to know," then it is doubtful that a UN Director General's efforts would be anymore effectual. We could also assume that the previous director, Javier Pérez de Cuéllar, had been sworn to secrecy after his encounter in Manhattan.

Furthermore, since there must have been at least a few other people who witnessed that startling event, they may have been paid a visit by the infamous 'men in black' who allegedly make sinister veiled threats to the observers. As well as that approach, they could simply be told that it was all a film company utilising their special effects technology, which would no doubt work as TV and film companies often shoot scenes in the open in those areas of the US.

With regard to the 'faceless group', and the devious methods they employ, it is quite surprising that they can defy the law with such impunity. It is quite worthless to release reams of paper that have most of the text obliterated and to make it clear that only they are privy to the actual information and that anyone else (including presidents) do not 'need to know.'

With regard to NASA and the space exploration activity and also the S.E.T.I Programme, it is not entirely the fault of NASA alone to be reticent about releasing information that they think may alarm the public; NASA itself was warned some time ago in the form of the so-called 'Brookings Report' that strongly encouraged NASA to be careful with regard to such information and how it should (or should not) be revealed to the public.

Also, the Brookings Institute was well aware how the general public can so easily be startled and panicked – this was evidenced by the reaction of many when they believed that a fictional radio programme about a Martian attack was true. The fact that the programme was fiction was stated at the start, but many people only switched on once the programme had started. It was based upon H G Wells' story about Martians out to conquer Earth, and focused on the rights of the people of the Earth. This contrasts with the potential reality that knowledge of such alien encounters is kept secret among a mysterious cartel who no one has elected. This group could well be in possession of data that many people may find too incredible to believe. Sometime after her abduction, Betty Hill said, "I was brought up to believe in what I suppose is called the scientific method. You don't believe in anything unless it can be dissected or put in a particular niche. I don't believe in ghost stories. Before this experience, my attitude was that if anyone believed in anything I don't understand, or that seemed too far out, I considered a sort of kook. Now, I think that I have more tolerance toward new ideas, even if I can't accept them myself." After what she went through, we are not surprised.

The close encounter of the third kind that was witnessed by Javier Pérez de Cuéllar did not become common knowledge for some time. Unlike anyone else who could have chatted about it freely, if de Cuéllar had spoken about it, he would certainly have had a visit from the mysterious MIBs, or Men in Black, and have been successfully silenced. De Cuéllar's observation took place in 1989, and it was obviously still on his mind in 1994 (five years later) when he is said to have discussed it with the Crown Prince of Lichtenstein, Hans Adam, who later stated that he had received veiled threats. Dr Stephen Greer was said to have revealed this information, also Dr Michael Salah PhD is said to have a website with all this information in it. Dr Salah often appears on TV editions of programmes that deal with cosmological mysteries, questions and events that pertain to extra-terrestrial events, including abductions that are definitely worldwide in nature. This would seem to indicate that the alleged abductions cover all ethnicities. It is also interesting to note that Betty and Barney Hill were a mixed-race couple. One of the questions that we must ask with regard to the existence of the Greys is, if they are the descendants of beings who were the creators of humanity via genetic interference, then they would surely be fully conversant with the human body and its biological makeup. Therefore, it seems that the human abductions may have a totally different purpose.

It has been seriously suggested that part of the Greys' agenda is to produce alien hybrids that are humanlike in all respects but have specially advanced powers and mental capacity (not necessarily for use in this world only). If their purpose was to breed out our least desirable qualities and our more negative modes of behaviour and influence our mental capacity, then these hybrids would also be useful. If two thousand years ago these beings were active on Earth, then they would certainly go unnoticed on Earth today. Since reproductive material was removed from both Betty and Barney Hill, then the offspring from their alleged abduction may be active in the world today or even somewhere far from it. There is no doubt that the Hills' case is the most compelling and believable of them all, but this should not be surprising with regard to the amount of publicity it received. We have said that the best account of it is contained in The Interrupted Journey by John G Fuller. This book is recommended for its attention to detail and because it relates much information that was revealed by the Hills when under hypnosis that came out on the tape recording which may well be still in existence. Barney did express a wish that they should be preserved in order to help others like him and his wife. Dr Benjamin Simon's objective was to release the amnesia they both had and to gradually reveal what experiences they had had during this time period. For all that, Dr Simon knew that they could simply have been asleep in their car. In fact, during the entire process, Dr Simon 'pressed' this point whenever possible in the hope of reinforcing his belief that they did fall asleep or that Barney simply 'inherited' the dreams that Betty had experienced afterwards, which were quite explicit.

Dr Simon's primary objective was to relieve them of the stress and apprehension that they had gone through, due entirely to the missing period of time, as it was having a detrimental effect on Barney and his health; his ulcers flared up during this period of stress whereas they had previously shown signs of clearing up. On top of all that, they had experienced periodic flashbacks, which is probably the brain attempting to recover memory. As we have said, their case may not have reached the full-blooded attention that it later received, were it not for the Look magazine that the Hills felt was a somewhat distorted account and they wished to correct this for the public.

The last thing the Hills had in mind was any publicity or fame, but just to remove any distorted information about the event. They could no longer tolerate or ignore the disturbing after effects of it all. Certainly, John G Fuller's book helped greatly with this, as it stuck so close to the facts and avoided any over dramatisation of the case.

There must be some very advanced type of equipment aboard the alleged alien craft of an 'up close' and optical nature as they appear to select their victims so carefully and also seem to be confident of being able to fully control them by and cleverly manoeuvring themselves and their victims into position. With regard to the Hills themselves, they could not have been a more sensible and down-to-earth couple who had a successful mixed marriage and were both employed in responsible positions. Betty was a social worker with a substantial caseload. Barney worked at a Post Office in Boston, but was also involved in civil rights issues. They were both respected in the community and involved with the United Reform Church. They led busy lives and were fully occupied. When they came under the control of Dr Ben Simon, they could not have been in better hands. As far as Dr Simon was concerned, his clients, the Hills, were to be treated for amnesia and not whether ETs appeared and abducted them or not. The 'missing time' syndrome was bothering the Hills, and this phenomenon prevails in all abduction claims. Dr Simon in his profession was a neuropsychiatrist and foremost in his additional skills as a hypnotherapist. He was a Fellow of the Rockefeller Foundation and had lectured at Harvard and Yale Universities, but he was not unfamiliar with the whole strange story that the Hills had to relate as he had checked them out. The Hills' experience occurred during a short trip at the end of the busy holiday period. Most venues, such as motels, visitor centres and so forth, were preparing for the winter that was fast approaching. The Hills chose to go on a short break to Canada and Niagara Falls, then work their way back to their home in New Hampshire. Betty, not having to concentrate on driving, was able to look about more and it was she who first noticed the moving white light that appeared to be getting larger and becoming closer flying in a somewhat erratic manner.

Betty's requests for Barney to stop and to get a better look at the object were beginning to irritate Barney, as she was inferring that it was a UFO. Barney offered every other explanation, such as a helicopter, a piper club, a passenger plane, even an Air Force jet. When they finally pulled off the road onto a viewing spot that was common on routes through the mountains, Barney got out of the car with a pair of binoculars and walked some distance from the car and looked at the object. It had by now come much lower and was clearly 'pancake shaped' as Barney later described it, and was tilted slightly toward him. When he focused in on it with the binoculars, he was dumbstruck and transfixed by what he saw, which was revealed in the hypnotic sessions. Barney saw a figure looking down at him; it had large black slanting eyes and seemed to be directing him in some way. It was looking at Barney from a lighted window; other windows seemed to be apparent around the circular craft and also living entities. During the hypnotic sessions, Dr Simon had to occasionally take Barney out of his trance as he was getting so excited and emotional. He was trying to jump out of his seat. Barney related how he desperately wanted to pull the binoculars down from his eyes, but couldn't muster enough strength to do so. Eventually, he managed to pull the binoculars away from his eyes with such force that he broke the strap and ran back to the car. Then threw the binoculars on the seat, shouting that they were going to be captured and must get away.

At this point Betty was not sure whether he was laughing or crying, but as they sped away Betty asked, "Well … now do you believe in UFOs?" Barney answered, "Don't be ridiculous." Shortly after they drove away, they both heard a series of 'beeps' that appeared to be coming from the rear of the car in the boot area. On the way home, knowing they were a couple of hours behind schedule, they may have considered the explanation that they spent too much time watching the antics of the 'plane.' But Betty certainly would not have used that description. When they finally got home, three strange things happened. When they were getting their things out of the car, Betty noticed a series of small disc-shaped spots on the trunk, what we would call the boot lid.

When they got inside the house, Betty removed her dress, folded it up neatly, and never wore it again. Barney went into the bathroom and examined his groin area; he noticed a circular formation of what looked like warts. All these things played on their minds and, in addition to the missing time, began to develop into a kind of paranoia. Another factor caused them concern, which was the urge to look out of the window, which they both did from time to time.

The difference in their attitude of mind toward the incident began to show itself. Whereas Barney wanted to bury it down deep, Betty wanted to continually chat about it. After they had rested, Betty was soon on the phone to her sister. Barney at this point found that he had a red welt on the back of his neck and he knew that he had broken the strap of the binoculars. Whereas Betty was convincing herself more and more that they had witnessed a UFO. Barney was trying, but not very successfully, to convince himself that they had not.

Barney was somewhat annoyed that during the whole process, at least the part they could remember, not a single truck, car or Police Patrol vehicle came by that they could have flagged down in order to corroborate and help to identify what they were seeing. Another thing that Barney noticed was that his shoes were scuffed. How could that have happened? However much Barney thought about the incident, he could not get past the point where he ran back to the car and heard the beeping noise coming from the boot of his car. It was also difficult for him to believe that he had not heard Betty's shouts for him to come back when he was a good distance from the car. Betty had asked him why he felt that they were going to be captured. Betty's sister had previously experienced a UFO sighting some years ago, and when Betty was on the phone to her, the incident came up.

Betty's sister's husband was an amateur astronomer and a nearby neighbour was a physicist and suggested that if the strange craft had come as low as it did, then they may have been subjected to some kind of radiation or contamination. Her sister must have visited the physicist neighbour and related the story to him because the suggestion was made and related to Betty in a later call, that if they had a compass, they should check out the car with it. Barney was against this, as he subconsciously did not seem to wish to have anything that may reveal their experience as real, whereas he was trying to suppress it all. Others were not. When Betty ran the compass over the car and came to the boot lid, she observed a series of shiny disc-shaped spots. There were around twelve of them and she described them as about the size of a silver dollar coin. When she put the compass by them, it spun erratically. Betty, in her excitement, wanted Barney to look at the reaction. Barney reluctantly did so but did not register that he was particularly impressed, just saying it was the metal car. Betty was quickly back on the phone to her sister who advised after consulting with a recently retired Police Officer, to call the local US Pease Air Force Base. The story was gradually spreading with more and more people chatting about it, which is exactly what Barney did not want, but when the Pease Air Force Officer had finished talking to her, he wanted to speak to Barney. Barney finally agreed after Betty's prompting and felt less sheepish and embarrassed after he realised that the Air Force Officer was not going to be cynical or dismissive (as he had learned so many of them were). Barney's 'antenna' was up, and he was not going to be treated as though he had imagined it all. However, when the officer made it clear, that he (Barney) was not the only one who had gone through such an experience, he began to feel more relaxed about talking about it although he still did not give out every detail of the event that he could remember.

Strangely, although it might have been helpful or relevant, neither Betty nor Barney thought of telling the Air Force Officer about the shiny spots on the rear of their car or mentioned the point where they had heard the beeping sounds, or that of the reaction of the compass needle when placed near them. It could have been important as they were received just before they stopped and this may have been some sort of force applied so that they would stop. However, Betty did mention the beeping sounds to another investigator, an ex-Marine Corps Major who was now a UFO analyst. He was head of a civilian investigative group dealing with the phenomena. Betty mentioned a second series of beeping noises at the point just before they witnessed the object departing.

At this point, both Betty and Barney simply assumed that they saw an object come down close to them and then depart. Betty thought it was a UFO, but Barney did not want to admit that. It was the significance of the second set of beeps that seemed to be the point when they were released from some kind of control and were allowed to go on their way. However, the two missing hours of time, or their 'double amnesia,' still had to be accounted for.

When talking with the Air Force Officer, as said Barney did not tell him everything, especially when looking at the object through the binoculars and how he could not seem to stop watching it or that he had ran back to the car with a feeling that something was going to capture them. Barney's fear of ridicule was the uppermost thought in his mind, but Betty was quite the opposite in her outlook. Perhaps it was (on her part) some kind of unrealised self-therapy, which would have been a better approach than bottling everything up inside. Her training as a social worker may have helped in this regard. To alleviate the stress caused by the amnesia, one of the things they often did was to drive out of the area and try to find the exact spot where they thought their experience had occurred. But they had little success in this and often disagreed on where it happened.

Although Barney did not seem to be too affected by vivid dreams regarding the traumatic encounters, the exact opposite was the case with Betty, although she did not want to discuss them with Barney. It was this factor that was really a weak point in Dr Simon's consideration that Betty had simply dreamt the whole thing and that Barney had somehow absorbed all the salient points of her dreams. Nevertheless, after all the therapy sessions, Dr Simon still felt that this was, in his mind, the only rational explanation for the whole event.

We would not like to suggest that he was closed-minded to the alternative explanation, as many scientifically minded people are, but dwell on the point that his only objective was to relieve their anxiety problems; when he had achieved that, he would consider his job done and whatever came out during his process of therapy was for the Hills to deal with. They would then be free to either accept or forget it. Betty continued in her (possibly unrealised) 'self-therapy' by discussing it with people that she felt she could trust, such as her social worker friends, one of whom advised her to write down everything upon awakening while it was still fresh in her mind. However, Barney could not help overhearing her various phone conversations when she was talking excitedly about it all with her friends.

The details Betty revealed were quite explicit, and it seemed as though her recall was improving all the time and that eventually she might not have needed any hypnotherapy at all. The mind is a very delicate instrument, as the neurologists tell us, and if it's given free rein, it will oblige. But if certain factors restrain it of a mental nature, then the only option is therapy.

It would seem that the unidentified 'force' that was applied to them was less intensely applied to Betty than to Barney, but their own brainpower would be a factor at play with regard to the amnesia. Although the cloud was thinning out somewhat with regard to Betty's recall, it did not seem to help much when they retraced their route and tried to locate the exact points where their memory seemed to fail them.

In her dreams, Betty recalled a kind of roadblock that one might encounter when coming upon a traffic accident. She also remembered short, dark figures approaching their car. Betty's dreams gave the impression that her experience was somehow being purposely revealed to her, as it will be shown that the data that came out on her tape recording showed her to have been quite accommodating to the alleged Greys by asking questions wondering where they came from and if they might return. On the other hand, Barney kept his eyes screwed up tight and felt animosity toward them, and just wanted to get away.

Betty, on the other hand, remembered (in her dreams) both herself and Barney being firmly supported and guided toward and up the ramp of some sort of craft. Betty was aware of Barney being helped along by other beings, but he seemed to be more subdued than Betty, who appeared to be taking in more detail. She even recalls his feet dragging along the ground. This point is interesting due to the fact (as we mentioned) Barney was quite puzzled when they got home about his shoes being scuffed 'on top' of the toe area. Quite a substantial amount of detail emerged due to the dreams Betty had over the months since their experience. And, because of this data (which emerged on Dr Simon's tape recordings), it was quite natural that Simon would develop his thesis that the events took place in Betty's dreams and that Barney could have picked up on them. In that regard, such detail ought to emerge in Barney's hypnotherapy. However, it did not turn out to be as simple as that, and Barney's account was confined largely to his own experiences and fear of what was happening to him personally.

Dr Simon did admit to trying every ploy he knew to reinforce his theory of absorption of Betty's dreams, but he could not break their story. If they had both related the same details almost word-for-word, then that would indicate that Dr Simon's theory was correct, but it was quite clear that their experience differed noticeably with regard to what happened to them in the 'operating room.'

We have said that during WWII, Dr Simon was a Lt. Colonel in the US Army, assigned to help so-called 'shell shocked' soldiers who were traumatised so badly that they could not function efficiently as fighting men. He was well aware, of course, that some of them could be 'faking it' in order to get out of frontline combat. Dr Simon became quite experienced in recognising the genuine cases. Although he did not completely abandon his 'dream absorption theory.' At the end of his hypnotherapy sessions that revealed a host of detail on the tape recording, Dr Simon could not help but believe that the Hill's experience occurred exactly as they believed in the way that it happened. This could mean, for example, that if a person was hypnotised into believing that a certain thing happened and was later subjected to the stress evaluation test, they would state it as a fact without the machine indicating a lie.

However, Dr Simon could not forget the point that after they pulled off the road to watch the strange object in the sky, that they had simply fallen asleep for an hour or two and each formulated their own dreams, thereby producing the different accounts. However, many things came out on the tape recordings that defied any conclusive assumption that Dr Simon had considered, but still did not eliminate them; he had to remain completely objective.

Barney had admitted to overhearing many of the phone conversations that Betty had made to the various people they knew and to have listened to her accounts of what happened to them in her dreams. So, for quite some time, the Hills tolerated uncomfortably all their disturbing thoughts, dreams and wonderment regarding their 'double amnesia' which apparently is quite rare, but eventually it all had to come to a head at some point by positive action on their part, as it showed no signs of abating.

Although they certainly had not intended it or wished for it, the story naturally spread because of Betty's (what we could call) self-therapy, in relating their story to so many of her friends and associates. As it happened, in that part of New Hampshire there had been a good many reports of UFO related events to the nearby Pease Air Force Base, which is why the Air Force Officer seemed to be more interested than derisive when Barney outlined most of the details of their experience and Barney had noted this. Also, the Hills were well known and quite respected in the area and no one could classify them as 'kooks' or some kind of publicity seekers. Also, it is most interesting to note, as will be mentioned later, that a UFO sighting was logged and recorded in the files of an investigative organisation dealing with the phenomena and that it occurred at the same time and in the same location as the Hills event. The Hills tolerated all the uncertainty for two years. Before that time, because of Betty's clearer recall of certain points in what happened in the White Mountains, plus her vivid dreams, she wanted to know more about the UFO phenomena that previously she had little or no interest in. As a result, she wrote to an authority on the subject.

At one point during their discussions between themselves regarding the incident, Barney suggested that they both go into separate rooms and sketch, as far as they could recall, what the craft they had observed looked like. The result was remarkably similar with regard to their drawings. As said, due to her developing interest in the UFO phenomena, Betty was curious whether other people had experienced anything similar to their encounter, and she came across a certain ex-marine major, Donald Keyhoe. Keyhoe was head of a research unit called NICAP, which stood for the National Investigative Committee on Aerial Phenomena. Betty decided to communicate with him by mail.

Donald Keyhoe was obviously intrigued by Betty's account, particularly as it involved someone who could not be lightly dismissed as an unreliable witness. Betty wrote out the whole experience in her letter, including the part she had not spoken about to others, which was that Barney actually observed figures in the craft. Barney had seen the figures before he dashed to their car, yelling about being captured. The beeps they received, that is the second set, must have been intended to produce their amnesia about the figures and the whole encounter. The first set, of course, induced them to drive off the road into the hands of the aliens, who had then landed their craft. We might pause here to note that claims of human abductions had risen into the hundreds of thousands and that a logistical survey ought to have been carried out in order to look for certain salient points, that may indicate some kind of pattern, established by computer analyses, (of course it may well have been done in secret). If it has, then one would expect to observe a plan or purpose for it all. One factor we could see beforehand would be the sheer numbers involved, which should tell us something.

Obviously, some things would be noted without an in-depth analysis. When running through the factors relating to the victims, such as male, female, height, age, eye colour, hair colour and numerous other factors. Oddly enough, one common feature did arise, which does not seem to make much sense on its own, and that was the colour of the eyes, which were predominately green/hazel type. In addition to this, there was some similarity in the blood groups of the victims, which was said to be the rare

Rhesus Negative factor. The average man in the street would not be able to deduce much from all these factors, but they may be significant to the biologists. We would have to ask how would the alleged Greys or alien abductors know beforehand that their proposed victims possessed these points in their makeup?

But, to return to the Betty and Barney Hill case, although after the event Betty was obtaining as much information as she could with regard to the UFO phenomena, she had previously had little or no interest in this topic. By contrast, Barney chose the opposite path and chose to try to forget about it all, but he could not erase from his memory his experience of viewing the aerial craft through his binoculars. The most shocking feature to Barney was the living creatures he observed looking down at him. Some kind of force prevented him from pulling down the binoculars and running away. It was the creature's eyes that seemed to exert this force, and Barney felt that through this force, it was trying to capture him. After finally breaking away and running to the car, it was then that they first heard the series of beeping noises. As said, this certainly indicates that the beeping noises were first to obtain control, and then to relinquish it after inducing their amnesia.

During hypnotherapy, much was revealed to Betty about what happened on the craft. Barney was largely free of this problem; no doubt due to his strong mental resistance to accept what happened to them. As said, their story, because of its interesting and unusual aspects, was becoming more widely known and not just in a localised area. Major Donald Keyhoe was most familiar with their case, as Betty had written to him and revealed all the details she could recall.

Other interested parties included Walter Webb of the Boston Planetarium and Richard Hall of NICAP, that is, The National Investigation Committee on Ariel Phenomena. We may also mention Betty's sister and the people she knew, such as the physicist and the Air Force Officer that Barney had spoken to. When discussing the case with Walter Webb in particular, the part where Barney had mentioned the living ETs that Barney saw looking down at him caused Walter Webb to become somewhat sceptical because of other reports of this type had become suspect.

But Walter Webb was reluctant to abandon his interest in the case because of the many other intriguing factors surrounding it and he decided to reserve his judgement for the time being. Eventually, he arrived at the home of the Hills in October 1961 with a determination to discover any obvious flaws in the case by his careful questioning, gleaned by many other 'close encounters of the third kind', that Dr J Allen Hynek introduced into the investigation process. When the interview began, Barney, who had come to realise that their story was not going to be treated with suspicion straight away, opened up a lot more than he usually would with regard to their experience. Walter Webb interviewed the Hills both individually and separately and, try as he did, he could not discover any obvious flaws, inconsistencies or contradictions in the intriguing story that they related, which he fully expected to find.

Walter Webb, in fact, was so impressed that he could do little else but to accept that the Hills were telling the truth. At this point, he realised that certain parts of the Hills story should prove to be very revealing if they could be brought out by a professional hypnotherapist.

The number of people involved either directly or indirectly with the Hills case continued to rise all the time. Perhaps because UFO investigative groups share salient points in their data with each other's teams. The next group of people who were intrigued by their story and contacted the Hills were Robert Holman and CD Jackson. When this group visited the Hills, it also included a retired US Air Force Officer who had worked in the intelligence branch of the Air Force. This was Major James MacDonald. The positive result from this interview, which we could assume was influenced by Walter Webb, was the suggestion made by Major MacDonald that Betty and Barney should agree to submit themselves to some kind of professional medical procedure involving hypnosis, but not by some stage entertainer but rather by a reputable therapist experienced in such matters.

The main objective of the process would be to unlock the amnesia or so- called (in modern parlance) 'missing time period,' that is common to all alleged alien abduction claims. The person they first contacted with regard to this case, after having studied details, felt that the best person to deal with their case was the gentleman that we mentioned earlier, Dr Benjamin Simon of Boston. It was in December 1963 that Dr Simon took on the task of dealing with their case. Barney Hill, having suffered for some time with ulcers, was the worst affected over the previous two years and the stress of wondering what Dr Simon would reveal did not help, but he had to go through with it for his own peace of mind.

Betty, on the other hand, who seemed less stressed about it all, was in a sense, actually looking forward to the coming hypnotherapy sessions. In their first session, Dr Simon hypnotised them separately and, after a few more sessions of separate treatment, finally brought them together for the process. All of the astounding details and emotions experienced as they relived them came out on the recordings.

At one point, when Barney was under therapy Betty, although in a separate room (that was not next door) could not help overhearing Barney's anguishing cries as he relived his experience, which disturbed her, but she made no mention of this to Barney later. She knew he was under hypnosis and would not remember it, as it was down to Dr Simon's decision when to reveal everything that came out on the tapes when he was ready to do so.

When Barney, under hypnosis, got to the point of relating all the prior data with regard to the events they experienced on their trip home back through the White Mountains, he eventually comes to the point where they both see an exceptionally bright 'star.' It soon became clear that what Barney was relating was not a star, but rather a very bright object that was obviously under some kind of control.

As all the information came from Barney's lips onto the recording tapes, it soon became clear to Dr Simon why Barney had become so badly affected in comparison to Betty; he concluded that the reason was his mental refusal to accept what the object was thought to be (by Betty at any rate). She seemed to have no trouble in deciding that it was most certainly a UFO, and her constant references to the object as such were beginning to irritate him. He was clearly in denial, and this came out on the tapes. At this point, he was wishing that a state trooper, a truck, or any kind of vehicle would come by that he could flag down and discuss it with, as he was feeling quite exposed and fearful as to what seemed to be developing.

Barney tried to convince Betty (but mostly himself) that it was a light plane, a 'Piper Cub', as he called it. At this point in his therapy, he wanted to wake up and became quite excited and obviously displaying fear, but Dr Simon chose to let him continue further. Barney stated that he had looked around for anything that may serve as a weapon and he reached into the car for a tyre wrench. When Dr Simon further prompted Barney into describing more about the craft, Barney stated that it was 'pancake shaped' and had a row of windows that curved around the side. He further related that a being within the craft was looking at him and having a strange effect on him. At this point, he had bolted and found himself back in their car and intending to drive away. For some reason, he turned off the road, which surprised Betty, and she asked him why he had done this.

Soon he began to relate that some figures were approaching them. He then says, "They won't talk to me, only the eyes are talking to me. They are telling me not to be afraid." Shortly, Barney begins to talk as though some time had passed. Barney speaks as though he's talking to Betty in general conversation on the way home and says, "Well … it looks as though we are getting into Portsmouth a little later than we expected." At this point, Dr Simon felt that there was little point in continuing as Barney had passed the point that was relating to his amnesia and decided to terminate this part of the therapy. Dr Simon knew that the amnesia had not yet been pierced, but it was early days yet and he knew that he would get to it when the time was right. So, Dr Simon arranged to meet them again at a later date.

The Hills eventually returned to Dr Simon's office on February 9th, 1964. During this session with Barney, after Dr Simon had put him in a deep trance, he again turned his questions as to what Barney had thought he had seen. When Barney began to describe the craft as 'spinning like a top', Dr Simon guided Barney back to the point where he had turned off the road and the figures that were approaching their car. Barney's tone began to register excitement again. He stated that he felt weak and that the beings were helping him out of the car. He began to relate, "My eyes are tightly closed, I don't want to be operated on, I seemed disassociated, I'm going up a slight incline, I'm being told to keep my eyes closed, my groin feels cold, I'm lying on something, I feel that something is in my ear. The 'eyes' come close to me."

At one point, Barney stated that he did manage to open his eyes for a moment and described seeing what looked like a hospital operating theatre. It was brightly lit, with a bluish hue all around. After a pause he said, "I'm getting off the table and I am grinning because I feel so relieved, now I am walking and being guided back to our car, then I see Betty, she is coming down the road, she seems to be smiling."

After a short pause, Barney says, "We saw the object going; it was like a huge, bright orange ball. It was beautiful." There is a strange occurrence here when Barney was still under hypnosis. He said, "Betty said to me, 'now do you believe in flying saucers?', I said, don't be ridiculous, of course I don't." He had just related his experience with the Greys, so why would he say that? But straight after that remark, he stated that he heard the second set of beeping noises so he must have been released from his control to have said that, as it was after the departure of the craft anyway, also they had started off home. At this point, this particular session was over.

Dr Simon decided at this time that the next session would involve Betty and that he would work on her version of their encounter. It transpired that her description of their experience concurred with everything that Barney had said except, of course, his experience with what he thought was an operating room. She could not have been aware of any details regarding that.

During her session with Dr Simon when under deep hypnosis, she told him of the part where Barney had walked some way from the car with the binoculars to look up at the craft and she related that she screamed out at him to come back, "He came running back and threw the binoculars into the back of the car, he was almost hysterical and tried to start up the car." Betty seem to omit some detail here as Barney had said that he wanted to drive away, but for some reason drove off the main route because Betty picked up her story again by saying, "I was afraid when I saw the men in the road, they started coming towards us, I got scared, I tried to get away out of the car, to run into the wood, but there's a man on each side of me and another two of them in front of me, I turn around and Barney is behind me." Whereas Barney had said he kept his eyes tightly shut (and was told to), Betty did not seem to be under such tight control.

Betty carried on about receiving what appeared to be 'mental' rather than verbal instructions, trying to calm her. Betty received some mental inputs about not being afraid, "We don't want to harm you, we just want to do some tests, be calm and you will soon be back in your car." Betty continues to describe how the Greys were taking her toward the craft. One would expect that it would be at this point where they would be at their most terrified and trying to resist being taken and it proves the effectiveness of the mental calming forces that the Greys applied to them. Betty continued in her statement to Dr Simon. "They are taking me up to the object. It is on the ground." She explained that there was a ramp up to the craft, and when she entered it, she made it clear that the object was circular by saying, "There's a corridor that leads 'around' to a room. They lead Barney past me. In the room, they put me on a stool. There is a machine with a big lens looking at my skin." This would appear to be a large magnifying lens to look at the pores in the skin.

Betty continued, "They scrape my arm," clearly, this test was to obtain skin cells for later close analysis, also after every test, they put away the samples in to some kind of cabinet array. Betty runs through a whole series of tests and examinations of various parts of her body, but the most painful (although only briefly) was the part where they inserted a long needle into her navel and she cried out in her discomfort, but the being that seemed be in charge of the procedure soon alleviated the pain.

This particular test is of interest when considering the following: such a test was not in force as a general medical practice at the time of this alleged abduction, but did later come into general use on Earth as a process for various tests and as a procedure for extracting eggs. An interesting factor with regard to this test, and quite possibly other tests and procedures, is that it may have been part of an information transfer process. If, as we suspect, the Greys are working behind the scenes with the secret group of humans who hold information on us, then they may have knowledge of advanced procedures in many areas. These areas might include genetics, biology, and medical science. For those who support the theory that the forebears of the Greys could have been responsible for our very origins, then they would be well aware of our negative qualities that mean we rush into battle for issues that could be resolved by jaw (jaw rather than war).

So, we hope any assistance in military help and technology would be prohibited, but of course, nothing is guaranteed. During all the alleged abductions, particularly those where dialogue between the victims and the perpetrators has occurred, there was never any criticism apparent to the victims with regard to human behaviour toward each other. Yet, this contrasts enormously with the early stages of the UFO phenomenon where 'alien visitors' continually warned the people who had these close encounters of the folly of mankind with their nuclear bomb tests and warlike behaviour. Since those receiving the dire warnings were mostly farmhands or local café owners etc, it seems clear the stories were contrived to reflect their own concerns about human behaviour.

During Betty's encounter, she asked many questions. If the Greys actually existed in her convincing case, they must have been quite impressed by her cool and calm demeanour. When Dr Simon felt that they had got all he could from this session, he halted the procedure and told her that she would not remember anything about this meeting until they next met. Both Betty and Barney had no idea of the content and details of all the information that they had revealed to Dr Simon on the tape recordings, but obtained some psychological relief in the knowledge that at last it would surely all be resolved.

At the next session, it seems that Dr Simon had decided to probe a little more into the communications aspect between her and the alleged Greys. After he had put Betty under hypnosis, he brought her to the point where she was communicating with the being who was doing the testing. She knew that there were other figures around, but this being, whom Betty referred to as the 'Doctor', explained that the conversation was not verbal but that the replies to her questions 'came into her head.' It seems at this point that the creatures had completed her tests and did not seem in any hurry to take her back to their car. The being told Betty that they had not yet finished with Barney. Betty was anxious to prove that this had actually happened to her and could probably imagine herself chatting to her sister about it. She asked the being who had conducted the tests on her, if she could have some artefact to take back with her in order to prove she had gone through this experience.

Betty looked around, noticed a 'book', and asked if she could have that. This will be seen as quite bizarre in a sense; one would not expect that such advanced beings would have worked with physical books but would rather have had everything in some form of advanced electronic form. However, there it was and strangely, the being seemed to agree that she could take it. But this seems odd. If they were so careful to induce amnesia, why would they give Betty something to prove the experience?

Betty must have taken hold of it as she explained that it had a lot of vertical lines or symbols (no doubt alien writing), however, she never managed to obtain the book. She related that the other beings seemed to intervene and there seemed to be some kind of excited chatter among the group. Eventually, the main man she called 'the doctor', explained that because the others objected to her taking it, he had changed his mind (one can imagine the cynics nodding at each other). If Betty had managed to secure the book, such an item would be priceless. Betty also related to Dr Simon that when the excitement died down, it seemed that something else had them all 'in a huddle,' so to speak. One of the beings had what appeared to be a dental plate held in what looked like forceps. Then the main 'man' came over to Betty and began pulling at her teeth.

The dentures belonged to Barney, so the rest of the group expected Betty's teeth to come out. This raised another strange factor; one would expect that the alleged Greys would have encountered other abduction victims who had dentures, but perhaps not. And in the early sixties, this may only have been the beginning of the ET's more intensive programme.

With regard to other factors that arose during Betty's abduction, she had trouble trying to explain the meaning of some phrases she used when conversing with 'the main man', such as 'old age.' And when Betty used the word 'time', they asked, "What is time?" Again, this is strange because the alleged abductors used this term telepathically themselves on occasions, such as, 'all in good time', or 'we'll have you back in your car in no time'. It is not known to this day whether any kind of implants were inserted into Betty or Barney, but this seems to be a feature of modern-day claims where a substantial amount of items have been removed from the victims. There was no reason to have carried out any X-ray on Betty or Barney at that time. However, the leader informed Betty that they could easily find them again if they so wished and this seemed to imply some kind of detection device had been inserted into them. To return to the closing stages of Betty's abduction, she told Dr Simon during hypnosis that she was very upset when she was told that she could not take the book. She then told Dr Simon how they began to lead her out of the examination room and out into the corridor, and Barney was being helped along behind her. Then, once again, they descended down the ramp and were back in their car.

Dr Simon did admit that he tried every trick he knew to try to trap them or make them subconsciously admit that they had fallen asleep in their car, but they never faltered in their story. Another factor with regard to the recall of both Betty and Barney was the noticeable difference in their accounts. Betty related quite a detailed amount of data and was quite explicit with describing her physical examination; Barney recoiled from it and hated it.

Whereas Betty could quite easily recall the various types of instruments used in the test and what they were used for, Barney's recall was quite vague. Under hypnosis, he remembered feeling a cold sensation when some kind of cup was placed over his groin area. Barney's experience of the process could not be more difference than Betty's. He did not wish to chat to them about it all and felt quite violated. This caused Barney to become very agitated and Dr Simon had to reinforce his hypnotic condition from time to time as he was shouting and trying to leave his seat. He made it clear that he did not like them touching him. One may think that it ought to have been Betty to have reacted in that way.

Another interesting factor is that when the Greys had completed their procedure with Betty and the aforementioned dialogue ensued while she was waiting for Barney's tests to be completed, she found herself chatting away with the Greys quite amiably. Betty was curious where they had come from and asked the being she had grown used to communicating with. At that point, this creature drew something out of the wall like a shade that could be pulled out to keep rain off a shop front. It turned out to be a star map and depicted on it were large and small circles with either dots or lines linking the various globes, which Betty assumed were either suns or planets.

The being asked Betty if she could point out our Earth on the map. Of course, Betty could not and told the being so, the being replied, "If you do not recognise your own world, then it is of little use me showing you where we are from." In John Fuller's book, The interrupted Journey, he pointed out that under further hypnosis; Betty could recall and even draw the star chart. This was subsequently analysed by a group of astronomers, and after intense scrutiny, it turned out that their home planet was in the star system 'Zeta Reticuli'!

In Dr Benjamin's session, Betty continued, that she kept up quite a dialogue with the 'main man' from her analysis and mentioned to him that she was quite fascinated by the experience she had gone through and wondered if it was possible to see them again. This, one would think, would have surprised the abductors as they quite probably expected a reaction more like Barney's.

However, with regard to the question that was asked by Betty, the Leader replied, "If it is possible, you will." To return to the 'book', Betty wanted, it may have been just a quick reference star chart or mission profile. But whatever it was, it would have been highly classified and not offered to Betty to take away. Barney, on the other hand, had no dialogue with the Greys and only vaguely recalled the procedure and then being finally supported in a semi-conscious state back to their car.

Clearly, Betty, with her obvious inquisitiveness, was a far easier subject to handle than Barney. Again, on completion of the tests, Betty said, "I do wish I really knew if you were going to come back." The Leader replied, "Well …. We will see." A little later, when they were both back in their car, Betty said to Barney, "Come on out, let's watch them leave," but Barney was still in a fog. The small dog they had with them on the trip cowered in a ball in their car and was still visibly trembling. This was all recalled by Betty during her hypnotherapy with Dr Simon.

She described the object as, "Getting brighter and brighter like a big orange ball." When Betty heard the beeping noises, she took it as some kind of farewell signal, but in reality, it was undoubtedly a process to reinforce their amnesia. In spite of all this detail, Dr Simon still retained the idea that Betty's vivid dreams and recall had all been absorbed by Barney, and he pressed this point when Betty was under hypnosis.

Dr Simon asked Betty, "Your memory is sharp. Now, did you at any time tell Barney all about your experience in the spacecraft?" Betty then answered, "No, because I sensed that Barney was determined to forget it." He then asked, "Did you sleep at any time during your trip?" And Betty was sure they had not. When all the sessions of therapy had been completed and recorded, certain factors that had puzzled them before now made more sense – especially after the tapes were played back to them. For example, the issue of why Barney's shoes were scuffed. During the playback of the tapes, this issue was cleared up for him when he heard himself relating how he was removed from the car. He realised that he was less co-operative with the Greys than Betty. It must have taken all the strength of the Greys to support him and get him into the craft. On the tapes, he heard himself saying that his shoes were scrapping over rocks before he was guided up the ramp. He then experienced how his feet bumped over a kind of bulkhead like one sees on ships.

In the examination room, Dr Simon asked Barney whether he could recall any kind of dialogue or speech among the entities during his examination. Barney heard himself telling the Doctor that he heard what sounded like a mixture between a humming noise and low buzzing tone. As a matter of fact, this same description is given in various other reports of alleged abductions and seems to be a common feature among them. And of course, the most common factor reported is their physical, grey-looking skin. This description has built up steadily over many years of these occurrences.

When Dr Simon had completed the sessions and re-analysed all the data obtained from the Hills, he was able to eliminate certain factors straight away; namely, that it was a complete fabrication, or that it was a dual illusion or hallucination. But when it came to the possibility that it could indeed have been alien life forms and technology, he baulked at the prospect of accepting this. The reason being that this type of experience had, in his opinion, never been documented reliably in research data.

We could raise a couple of issues here. Some people, although highly intelligent and qualified, can never allow themselves to step over a certain line with regard to a subject they could not possibly accept. It is called, 'psychological purblindness.' Dr Simon had no intention of doing anything other than taking on their case to relieve the effects of their double amnesia. In this, he felt that he had been quite successful.

Another point that we would mention is the statement made by Dr Simon that "such cases had never been reliably documented." This is simply not so. There had already been very thorough analysis and documentation carried out, although it was 'early days' in the abductions. Dr J Allen Hynek had also reliably documented the subject. But Dr Simon had no interest in the theory of ETs on Earth, so he was not really in a position to state that the subject had never been reliably documented.

Nevertheless, he would not be human if he did not find what emerged from his work with the Hills intriguing, to say the least. Before reaching any final conclusion, he continued to consider the dream transference theory. And one trick question he tried was to ask Barny, "When you were stopped in the road by some men in black clothes, how did you learn of this experience?" Instead of saying, as Dr Simon might have expected, "Betty told me," he said, "I was hypnotised by Dr Simon." This clearly shows that Dr Simon had caused him to recall the event under hypnosis, and that he did not learn of this from Betty.

So, Dr Simon had to admit that the ploy had failed. Barney could not help but know of Betty's dreams because, as we have said previously, he had overheard her discussing them with her sister. But no mention of Barney's experiences could have been heard when Betty was recalling her dream experiences with her sister because she did not know about them. Barney's personal experiences only emerged when under hypnosis. Barney never wanted to discuss any dreams he had experienced with anyone except

Dr Simon and only then, if he was asked or if he could remember them. Betty had been encouraged to write down all the details of her dreams on awakening, but Barney never bothered with any of that.

When Barney was in his hypnotic trance, Dr Simon (still pursing the dream transference theory) asked him, "How about the other things that you described to me about what happened to you when they were examining you …. did Betty tell you about all that?" Barney answered, "No, she never told me, I was lying on the table and I felt them examining me." Dr Simon asked, "Is this part of Betty's dream?" Barney answered again quite firmly, "I am telling you what actually happened to me." Dr Simon still pursuing his point, "Now, about all this 'dream', about being taken on board and all the details in regard to it, this was all told to you by Betty wasn't it?" Barney answered, "No Betty never told me." Dr Simon then asked, "How do you know that all of this happened?" Barney replied in factual terms, even though he knew he was talking to Dr Simon and said, "I was hypnotised by Dr Simon and I told him what actually happened to me."

All of this clearly indicates that it was brought out of the repressed area of his mind that he had not wanted to believe, which is what the hypnotherapy was supposed to do. Dr Simon's primary objective, as said, was to lift the veil of their double amnesia, which it did, but one cannot simply turn one's back on the profound data that emerged along the way.

It would be interesting to know, if science has looked into what possible link there could be with the connections of the beeping sound and affecting the brains of Betty and Barney and also the shiny shaped marks on the area of their car where the noise emanated from, and if any secretive experiments have been tried to replicate them.

This is possible, as so much publicity in magazines, films and written accounts, such as in John G Fuller's book, exists regarding the Hills case. It has almost certainly been scientifically 'picked over' – no doubt with the results being highly classified. It was said that Barney himself wanted the tapes preserved in a secure environment to help future abduction victims. This was despite the fact that at first, before his hypnosis, Barney wanted to deny what had occurred and theorised instead that it had been a satellite, an Air Force jet or even a Piper Cub that they had seen. But the hypnosis enabled his mind to become unconstrained. During one part of the eventual recordings, Barney said, "I knew that I had seen a UFO, and that I got out of my car and walked towards it, I couldn't believe it was there and I couldn't make it go away. I felt compelled to go closer. I prayed for the strength to run back to my car and I did, but the 'eyes' kept following me and I felt very upset."

When all this occurred at the time of its recording, Barney was sobbing and so upset that Dr Simon felt he had to take firm action to control him. He repeated calming words forcefully, and Barney was then able to continue with his narrative. He described rushing back to his car, but instead of quickly heading for home after driving off, he said, "I made a turn off, I never knew the reason why, we were in a strange area, I felt very uncomfortable, the 'eyes' were telling me I should be calm, I saw men coming toward me."

It is easy to imagine a person being influenced and controlled by some strong character with piercing eyes directing someone with fairly weak resistance. But once eye contact has been broken, it is strange for a pair of eyes to remain in one's head and still direct that person. Dr Simon worked over a few sessions, continually repeating certain aspects of the story. At one session, Dr Simon again asked Barney, "Did you dream this?" Barney replied, "No, I did not dream it, I tried to get out of my car, I was supported by two of them, my eyes were closed." Dr Simon asked again, "Did Betty tell you this?" and Barney replied, "No Betty never told me this." Dr Simon asked Barney, "Do you think it really happened?" Barney answered, "It did happen. I don't want to remember it. I was told in my mind that I would forget that it happened." Dr Simon then reiterated, "Are you sure this really happened?" Barney firmly replied, "I feel very sure that it happened." Clearly, it seems that Barney had no doubt in his mind.

Dr Simon asked Barney, "Did these beings speak to you in words?" Barney answered, "I was told what to do by his thoughts. He told me that I wouldn't remember any of this. I wanted to forget it and he helped me to forget it. I knew something had happened. I was confused. I was driving back to Route 3 and wondered why I had gone off it. Shortly after that, we heard the beeping sounds."

When Dr Simon got back to Betty and put her under hypnosis by using the codeword that he used for her, which was different to that used for Barney, he found that her recall was as strong, if not stronger than that of Barneys. In fact, he was impressed by the similarity of the details that came forth, in particular when their experiences took place in separate rooms that each of them could not have known about.

For example, Barney could not remember the point when the beings removed his dental plate but Betty on the other hand, could plainly recall (and Dr Simon had it all on tape) the 'buzz' of excitement among the beings when one of them came in with Barney's dental plate and all the others gathered around it.

Examples such as this all tend to reinforce the authenticity of the case, but it seems to have had little effect on Dr Simon's opinion, which still centred around his belief in the dream transference possibility. Eventually, Dr Simon interviewed, and then hypnotised, both Betty and Barney together. Yet again, no inconsistencies arose. When it came to the point where the tapes were played back to both Betty and Barney, they were, to put it mildly, quite astounded and could hardly believe that it was themselves speaking. This, of course, is quite common when one hears their own voice on tape.

However, it was clear to Dr Simon that the process had been quite successful in the objective of having relieved their double amnesia, which was the whole reason for Dr Simon taking on their case. Dr Simon was aware that dreams can be confused with reality, but over time, the person gradually accepts that the experience was, in fact, a dream. It is estimated that dreams only last for a duration of six to seven seconds, so, for such an abundance of detail to reveal itself in both Betty and Barney, the possibility that they dreamt it all can be safely ruled out.

We have mentioned that recently, a medical surgeon named Dr Roger Leir who specialises in the medical procedures of patients who are in trauma due to alleged abduction experiences, has indicated that the X-ray plates taken clearly show small items in the flesh that ought not to be there. As mentioned, the objects proved to be composed of material contained in meteorites. But the odd part of it (if it was not odd enough) is that the items seem to have been treated in some way in order to prevent the human body from attempting to reject them. Of course, these processes were not in place at the time of Betty and Barney Hills encounter, or even considered as there was no obvious need for any X-ray procedures, but as we have said, the beings made it clear that they could easily find them again if they so wished. Perhaps this should have raised a few questions. Of course later, when some abduction victims claimed that they had been abducted again, the penny finally dropped (although it had mildew on it) that the abductions must have inserted some kind of homing device in their victims in order to locate them again.

There are a few questionable items that could be picked up on among all the data that came out on the tapes. One of these is the question of the 'book'; one would ponder why such things as 'books' would be still utilised by such advanced beings. Another oddity is that the entities apparently needed the aging process explained to them. This came about with the question that the entities had over why Barney's teeth came out and Betty's did not. Betty said that she explained that when people age, they sometimes lose their teeth and therefore require dentures. Another thing they asked Betty was, "What is time?" It seems that they were trying to find out how we humans conceive of such things as 'age' and 'time'.

Another strange thing is that at one point, the entity said the words "Wait a minute." This is curious because when using a telepathic process, the word 'minute' would only represent a period of time, such as we may say, 'jiffy'. It was presumably interpreted by her brain's evaluation process as a 'minute'. These alleged beings' concept of time must be vastly different to our worldly twenty-four-hour concept of it. They travel through it, across it, and must use it in ways that we can only make futuristic theories about.

Recently, a number of TV programmes have appeared about abductions, and the phenomenon is experiencing somewhat of a renaissance. One programme concentrated primarily on the enormous number of worldwide abduction claims that would clearly be of some concern to the psychiatrists and neurologists if they are all to be considered false.

In some cases, the same hypnotic regression processes were applied as in the Hills' case. But in other cases, this process may not be affordable to the victims, or victims may prefer to put it all down to a realistic dream and try to forget about it. If all cases are factual, then the Greys would know more about the human bodily systems than any of our own biologists or geneticists. This raises a more serious consideration which is "Why?" What is the ultimate purpose of it all? It seems to be a major 'creative' operation.

One easy way of explaining it is simple curiosity on the Greys' part about human anatomy – anatomy that may have been created by their forebears a long time ago. If the latter is the case, then this would make the human entity a kind of 'inherited intellectual property.' Therefore, the current Greys have a big problem. As they traverse the globe, they would see evidence of totally unacceptable behaviour on our part, and therefore a sense of failure on theirs. What should be done when humans, who have been bestowed with such advanced capabilities, continue to kill each other in constant wars? This cannot help but be a major topic of discussion among the hierarchy of the Greys wherever that might be.

One interesting point about the Hill's case is their health insurance. We mentioned that some victims of the alleged abductions have not been able to afford hypnotic regression sessions. In the Hills' case, they made a health insurance claim for their hypnotherapy sessions with Dr Simon. At first, the Medical Director of the insurance organisation was, quite naturally, reluctant to accept a claim involving the subject of a UFO encounter. They therefore required firm backup from the Hills' medical therapist. When Dr Simon replied with all the relevant information pertaining to the Hills' case and their anxiety and emotional disturbance, the insurance claim was promptly settled. This was, therefore, likely the first time an insurance claim was settled on the basis of a UFO abduction claim.

It may have been that the Hills' case may never have come to light at all, except that a Boston newspaper reporter had part of the story printed in his column. The Hills had not given their permission for this, but perhaps he escaped a lawsuit because it may have been classified as a human-interest story. However, the Hills wished to put the record straight and correct the account of certain distortions. When John G Fuller's book The Interrupted Journey came out, everything to do with the Hills case was put straight.

John G Fuller and Dr J Hynek met with Dr Simon. When Dr Hynek familiarised himself with all the details of the Hills' case, he made a review of his case files and discovered that a UFO report had been filed with the US Air Force showing that a radar contact with a UFO had been made. This report indicated that the UFO was in the exact vicinity where the Hills had experienced their close encounter. This, of course, if further corroborating evidence in support of their case.

Who could envy anyone who believed that they had been through the trauma of an alien abduction? The natural reaction of most people in conversation with such a person would be to avoid any deep discussion, or to avoid the person altogether. The person would have to deal with it mostly on their own. At least with Betty and Barney Hill, they had the advantage, not only of being able to support each other, but also to have the interest of some qualified people who could get them the help they needed. But a single person who had no reference points or factors to back them up would have severe problems mentally, with flashbacks, nightmares and the constant fear of their captors coming back for them.

Such people would have their everyday life disturbed. After such trauma, they would find it difficult to go about their normal work because it would always be uppermost in their mind. The worst effects, obviously, would be of a mental nature. Who could they trust or turn to? Who would believe them? Their best option would be to secure the services of a UFO investigation group. But the group would have to investigate the case thoroughly in order to be convinced of the genuineness of the claim, rather like a solicitor taking on a case. But an organisation dedicated to these matters would have the right connections to help; connections such as US Air Force Officers, physicists, doctors of astronomy, medical practitioners, etc.

But too many evidently have to deal with this on their own. One has to wonder if, or how many people who are incarcerated in mental institutions are there because of such encounters. Such experiences may have caused them to display symptoms of mental illness, and some may even have convinced themselves that this is where they belong. As said, it was quite a different situation for the Hills. They seemed (eventually) to get all the help and support that they needed.

It seems that the many thousands of people who claim to have been abducted will only be vindicated if or when a culminating point is reached with regard to it all; the point that we have called an 'end game.' But who will decide when this momentous event of realisation and revelation – that ETs have been among us for so long – will occur for humanity?

If we return briefly to the lone 'abductee' wondering who to turn to for help, consider the plight of one of the (fictitious) characters in my book, The Second Coming. The person in question, a middle-ranking army officer working as an aide to a senior general, returning with some coffee he had been sent out for, heard voices coming from the general's office when he knew he was alone. When softly opening the door, the general was speaking to a holographic image of an 'alien' suspended in mid-air. The general was relating secret defence measures from a classified file. The officer took what he had witnessed it to the top. When he returned from leave after being thanked and assured it would be attended to, he found that procedures were in place to incarcerate him. If this actually occurred in reality, then certain people in the secretive group would be entirely capable of such character assassination and having someone who today may be described as a 'whistle blower' certified or even employing such people as the 'men in black' to threaten them or worse.

Some people claim that there are signs that the 'end game' and profound revelations are close at hand. And, moreover, that we are slowly being (unconsciously) prepared for it through the media. TV channels are awash with programmes dealing with ancient astronauts, abductions, Biblical events, UFOs, conspiracy theories, messages alleged to be evident in the crop circles, and so-forth. On top of this, as we have mentioned, in at least one abduction claim, the perpetrators informed a lady victim that their earthly operations were 'drawing to a close.' Any many will exclaim, "Well it's about time!"

The 'faceless few' who have got away with retaining so much information from general release for so long have much to answer for, but no doubt they have prepared their plans and escape routes, and will avoid being brought to book.

The ancient fear of the unknown that is inherent in the human was reinforced when the Robertson panel and such organisations as the Bookings Institute firmly warned NASA to be wary about releasing whatever they discovered in space. Almost certainly, the SETI team has been similarly warned. All of this secrecy will, of course, make any revelations even more traumatic when they do eventually come out. In order to undo all that, we have suggested that the Church be given the role of strongly preparing the masses. Perhaps the best people for this would be figures such as Father William T Fulcopiod and the Reverend Barrow H Downing who happily accept the extra-terrestrial hypothesis and the fact that a second coming may be somewhat different from the Biblical version.

The greatest problem the Greys may have is how to reveal all to the masses. In this endeavour, they could work with the faceless ones by revealing all – not to presidents, prime ministers or to the people – but instead to a select group of ecclesiastics. In this way, ecclesiastics, who are already trained in pastoral care and at least have a precedent for ET involvement in humanity from thousands of years ago in the form of the Bible, could help humanity to come to terms with these profound and shocking revelations. They could formulate the greatest sermon of their lives in such a way that humanity would actually look forward to a 'second coming' and the further profound revelations that would inevitably occur.

THE END

Bibliography

Ashpole, E. *The Search for Extra-terrestrial Intelligence*. Blandford Press, 1990.

Asimov, Isaac. *Extra Terrestrial Civilisationa*. Robson Books, 1980.

Collyns, Robin. *Did Spacemen Colonise Earth?* Mayflower Books, 1975.

Ditfurth, Von, Hoimar. *Children of the universe: The Tale of Our Existence*. Allen & Unwin, 1975.

Drake, W. Raymond. *Gods And Spacemen in the East*. Sphere, 1974.

Eisley, Loren. *Darwin's Century*. Doubleday Anchor, 1958.

Flindt, Max H., Otto O. Binder. *Mankind Child of the Stars*. Cornet, 1999.

Fuller, John, G. *The Interrupted Journey*. Corgi, 1981.

J & C Bord. *Life Beyond Earth*. Gratton, 1992.

Leaky, Richard. *The Origin of Humankind*. Phoenix, 1996.

Leonard, George H. *Someone Else is on the Moon*. Sphere, 1976.

Moore, Ruth, E. *Evolution*. Time-Life International, 1971.

Noorbergen, R. *Secrets of the Lost Races*. Hodder & Stoughton, 1979.

Ridpath, Ian. *Messages from the Stars: Communication & Contact with Extra-Terrestrial Life, A Scientific View*. Fontana, 1978.

Sagan, Carl. *Cosmos*. Macdonald Futura Publishers, 1981.

Shapiro, Robert. *The Human Blueprint: The Race to Unlock the Secrets of our Genetic Script*. Cassell, 1992.

Spencer, John. *Gift of the Gods? Are UFOs Alien Visitors or Psychic Phenomena?* Virgin Publishing, 1994.

Spencer, John, and Hilary Evans. *Phenomenon: From Flying Saucers to UFOs Forty Years of Facts and Research*. Futura, 1988.

Steinhäuser, Gerhard, R. *Jesus Christ Heir to the Astronauts*. TBS The Book Service Ltd, 1974.

Stoneley, Jack, and A. T. Lawton. *Is Anyone Out There?* W. H. Allen, 1975.

Tomas, Andrew. *We are not the First*. Sphere Books Limited, 1972.

Trinkaus, Erik. *The Neanderthals*. Jonathan Cape, 1993.

Milton Keynes UK
Ingram Content Group UK Ltd.
UKHW020232250424
441687UK00002B/131